CCNA ROUTING AND SWITCHING

Routing and Switching Essentials for Beginners

Ethan Thorpe

Table of Contents

Introduction 1

Chapter 1: An Introduction to Cisco.............................5

Facts about Cisco 7

Differences between CCNA and CCNP..........................8

CCNA and CCNP Certification Training by Specialist 9

Chapter 2: Products and Services Offered by Cisco Networking Solutions...11

Networking 11

Product by Company Type...18

Services 18

Chapter 3: About CCNA Examination 19

Chapter 4: Different Types of CCNA Exam...................23

CCNA Routing and Switching 23

CCNA Cloud..23

CCNA Collaboration 25

CCNA Cyber Ops...26

CCNA Data Center..27

CCNA Industrial..28

CCNA Security 29

CCNA Service Provider.. 30

CCNA Wireless 31

Chapter 5: About CCNA Routing and Switching 33

The CCENT Examination 36

Cisco Certified Network Associate - Routing and Switching
(CCNA Routing and Switching) 37

Where Do You Take your Exam?.............................. 40

Always Use the Material Provided by Cisco Authorized
Publishers 42

**Chapter 6: Why Should You Appear For the CCNA Routing and
Switching Examination...43**

Certification is the Foundation That Networking Careers
Are Built Upon 44

Certification Gives You a Full Range of Training Options......... 44

Certification Gives You More Career Options 45

Certification Keeps You Current on All the Latest Technology
Changes 46

Learning Curve... 47

Certification Helps You Learn from Your Peers...................... 48

You'll Be Certified by the Networking Leader 48

Certification Helps Increase Your Paycheck 48

Don't Forget: There Is Value in Recertification 49

Certification Prepares You for Network Evolution in the
Digital Era... 50

Secure Your Career through Routing and Switching.............. 50

Globally Accepted.. 51

Certification Helps You Stand Out with Your Employer 52

Unique Way of Learning 52

Less-Extensive Outline 53

The Changing Role of Core Network Engineers........................ 54

Chapter 7: The Simplest Way to Earn the Certification 56

Basics of the CCNA Routing and Switching Certification 57

Exam Preparation 59

Recertification... 61

Chapter 8: Frequently Asked Questions and Myths 62

FAQ 62

Myths about CCNA... 66

Things to Keep in Mind 68

The Cisco Networking Fundamentals 70

Exam Objectives.. 71

Network Fundamentals 72

Operation of IP Data Networks 74

LAN Switching Technologies 75

IP Addressing – Ipv4 and IPv6.. 76

IP Routing Technologies 77

IP Services 78

Network Devices Security 78

WAN Technologies... 79

Infrastructure Services... 80

Infrastructure Security.. 81

Infrastructure Management 82

Chapter 9: Required Learning Material for Your CCNA Routing and Switching **84**

Look Out for Free Material 84

Your Peers are Your Greatest Resource 85

Mix It Up 85

Keep Yourself Updated 85

Get Practical... 86

The Cisco Official Study Material... 86

Self-Study Materials 87

Training 92

Cisco Official Course Material for Purchase 95

Chapter 10: Exam Tips **96**

Organize a Study Space 96

Get Involved in an Exam Prep Course 97

Create Your Own Custom Study Plan 97

Take Practice Exams 99

Transport Layer.. 102

Link Layer 102

Study Until it Feels Like Second Nature................................... 102

Give Yourself a Breather.. 103

Internet Layer 104

Join the Online Community 104

Revise... 105

Understand TCP/IP Stack Addressing & Data Flow 105

Have a Basic Understanding of the Cisco Command Line
Interface (CLI) 106

Get to Know Your Exam 106

Obtain the Right Material 107

Get Practical and Theoretical Experience 107

Never Rush to Take the Exam 108

Use Practice Drills and Flashcards 108

Have an Exam Day Preparation Plan 109

Strategic Tips 113

Chapter 11: Exam Study Plan 116

Week 1 117

Week 2 118

Week 3 120

Week 4 120

Important Concepts to Learn 121

Chapter 12: Cisco Recertification 124

Certification Policy of Cisco 125

Chapter 13: Sample Interview Questions and Answers 130

Conclusion 148

References: 150

Introduction

I want to thank you for choosing this book, 'CCNA Routing and Switching - Routing and Switching Essentials for Beginners.'

If you are someone who works in the IT industry, you will have definitely developed some love for the digital age. You would have also been interested to learn more about networking. The World Wide Web has changed the way the world operates and the best part is that it is available to us at the click of a button. With the advent of technology, there is a need to produce, upload, stream and download necessary data from the Internet, and this has become something that every single person does. So, do you know how this works? Most people use this technology regularly, but very few are aware of how the process works. There are some who want to learn more about the process, but would prefer to sit in the background and continue to use the Internet.

The best thing about these users is that they not only study the process, but they also spend some time to build this network for you. They work on some intrinsic products that you would love to use. You may be focused on using different products like Google, YouTube, etc., while the network and software professionals work on improving your experiences.

There are times when you may have wondered how some platforms function and work with large volumes of data. It is because of these networking and software professionals that this is possible. They work on building networks, connections and servers that will help us store our data with ease.

It does sound very simple, but it is anything but that. These professionals put in a lot of effort to improve different processes. The IT industry in the US holds a valuable place in the GDP contribution of the nation. Of the $3.8 trillion of US GDP, the IT sector accounts for $1.4 trillion and provides over 105 million jobs in the country. The IT sector has been contributing a whopping 14.6% growth in the GDP since the year 2014. It is true that the US is in the lead when compared to other countries in creating and supplying the most advanced hardware and software all around the world.

The role of a network engineer is the most sought after role in the IT industry. A network engineer is responsible for installing, supporting and managing the network and computer systems that keep the information going. They also play a crucial role in designing, implementing and maintaining network hardware and software solutions and also troubleshooting problems that arise in network installation and maintenance. They also ensure network safety, security and help maintain performance standards in the organization.

The changing economic times are creating a challenge for organizations, as every organization works on trying to retain its employees or wants to hire new network engineers who can maintain and optimize the existing systems. These individuals will also work on reducing costs thereby increasing the productivity of the employees in the company.

A company will always try to strengthen, improve or identify its competitive advantage, and it does this by implementing new network technologies that create opportunities for network administrators and network engineers to install, optimize and secure the newly installed systems. There is a huge demand for a network engineer in today's market, and this is not because of the economy. The economy has helped to increase the number of opportunities that an individual has as a network engineer. It has even taken on the moniker of a 'recession-proof career.'

If you are keen on giving your networking skills a try and turn it into a job or a passion, you should try to work as a network engineer since that is the apt job for you. The easiest way for you to do this is to join any company that hires networking engineers, especially the best companies, and work hard to find your path to success. Since there is a demand for network engineers, it is important that you advance your career in this domain. You can take up different courses that offer degrees in this field or specialize in training you in some areas of this field. One of these certifications is the CCNA program. When you take this course, you can certify yourself as a CCNA associate and this will open numerous opportunities in the world of switching and networking.

This book has been designed to help you understand what the basic requirements are for you to qualify as a CCNA Trained associate. You will also be taken into the world of Cisco to learn more about the numerous products and services they offer. It is important for you to learn this to enhance your understanding about CCNA. It is known that even with the necessary certification, knowing your company inside and out will help you to secure the job of your dreams. Your organization will see that you are making an effort to work on making it easier to solve problems. You can do this not only in the department you work in, but also in other departments where your skills can be used.

When you practice the methods that are mentioned above, you will notice that you are rising above your colleagues in no time. This book will also answer some questions that have been raised about the CCNA routing and switching examination. This book answers some of the frequently asked questions and also answers some concerns that are often raised about this examination. You will also learn more about why you need a certification, what the different CCNA exams are, how to attain certification for each and what exams can be taken to get the certification. This book also includes some tips and tricks that you can use to ace your test. It will also bust some myths about the examination.

Thank you once again for choosing this book and I wish you loads of luck in your journey to become a successful network engineer. I hope you find the book informative and helpful to learn and understand about CCNA successfully. The primary idea behind this book is to help you acquire your certification in the exams and become a Cisco certified network engineer. So, without any further ado, let us get started and get into the journey of learning all about CCNA.

Chapter 1

An Introduction to Cisco

The Cisco Networking Company was founded in the year 1984 by Leonard Bosack and Sandra Lerner. They began this company because they wanted to remain in touch with each other. They graduated in the year 1981, and began working at Stanford. Each of them led one computer department at Stanford. They learnt how to connect their computers to a network using a technology called router technology, which was devised in the year 1970. They later realized that they could create a router technology that could span across different departments, and believed that this would be a profitable business outside of the University. That is when, in the year 1984, the couple founded a company called Cisco Systems. It was after this that Cisco Systems received its first business – Stanford gave its proprietary software rights to Cisco Systems.

Cisco's first huge success was in the year 1985, when it sold its first product. This product is known as the Interface Card. This card was used by Digital Equipment Corporation to serve different network protocols that were introduced in the year 1986. The company needed cash for its expansion, which was offered by a venture capital firm called Sequoia Capital. It was then that things began to change for the founders. Sequoia Capital took over the company and decided to place John Morgridge as the CEO of the company. He did do a good job as the CEO, but did not want to work closely with the founders because it was difficult for him. When the company went public, the board removed Lerner, and soon Bosack also quit.

In the year 1993, Cisco introduced a new router, and also began to acquire some companies. The company first acquired Crescendo Communications that gave Cisco access to different network switching technologies. The company then relocated its headquarters from Menlo Park, California to San Jose after Morgridge was replaced by John T Chambers as the CEO. The company only began to acquire other companies since the CEO believed that you could only grow by acquiring competitors. In 1998, Cisco bought Selsius Systems, an Internet expertise company that helped Cisco take a dominant position in the VoIP technology industry.

In the year 2006, TelePresence, the first video conferencing tool was introduced by Cisco. This allowed people from across the globe to interact with each other. It made them believe that they were in the same room. Cisco Networking Enterprises eventually became the leading power in what is now called IoT or the Internet of Things. This gave companies a chance to shift from focusing only on hardware to software.

The history of Cisco is what made it what it is. That being said, the products and services that are offered by this company have made it a leader in the IT industry. The next chapter will list the different products and services offered by the company.

Facts about Cisco

It may be impossible for you to believe that love was the reason why Cisco was developed. Leonard Bosack and Sandra Lerner, the couple who created Cisco, wanted to make sure that they could stay in touch via email. This meant that they would need to connect numerous networks together. This led to the invention of a multi-protocol router, which was the first one of its kind. The saying, "necessity is the mother of all invention" couldn't be more apt. The first product of Cisco called the AGS Router was first shipped two years after the inception of Cisco. Does the name Cisco sound oddly familiar to you? The name Cisco was taken from the city of San Francisco which is the the trade and financial center of the US. Have you ever looked closely at Cisco's logo? If yes, did you notice that the logo was inspired by the Golden Gate Bridge? The name and logo of Cisco is derived from the city that the creators adored.

It was in 1990 that the company went public, which means that the creators were no longer the owners. When this happened, Lerner was fired from her job, and Bosack quit to show his solidarity with her. The founding members moved away, and they sold about 2/3rd of their stake in the company for $170 million. The estimated value of those shares today runs in billions, and as of 2014, 2/3rd of Cisco's share stood at a market value of a whopping $90 billion! The last reported revenue for Cisco was $49.3 billion.

Cisco has always acquired companies, and the first company that it acquired was Crescendo Communications in the year 1993. It has now acquired about 170 companies in total. Cisco also acquired ParStream and Lancope to expand upon its plan of "Security Everywhere."

Cisco has reached a large audience, and there are close to 72,000 employees in the company. It is present in over 360 locations across 160 countries and has close to 72,000 channel partners.

Differences between CCNA and CCNP

Both the CCNP and CCNA certifications are considered to be the most sought after certifications in the IT industry. There are some differences between the two certifications based on the level or the experience of the individual.

CCNP and CCNA stand for Cisco Certified Network Professional and Cisco Certified Network Associate respectively. An individual working in the IT industry is aware of these certifications since every organization values an employee with these certifications. Regardless of which certification you choose to appear for, you will need to appear for a written examination, which you must clear. There is also a lab examination conducted which will test your skills. The individual's expertise is only assessed after five rounds of tests. Each round will define the individual's expertise.

The CCNA examination also ensures that you will have a good understanding of buttoned and medium-range router systems, and can work with them easily. If you have this certification, and the necessary skills, your employer will know that you can install and activate the different systems in the network. In the same way, the CCNP certification will let employers know that you can work with and maintain area networks, like LAN and WAN, and can work with advanced solutions like voice, security, and wireless.

CCNA and CCNP Certification Training by Specialist

There are some prestigious positions that an individual can take up in the IT industry and they are the network engineers or system engineers. An individual with either the CCNA or CCNP certification is eligible for these roles. The CCNA examination also teaches you about security threats, wireless ideas and how systems can connect to the WAN or wide area network. You will also need to learn more about different protocols like SLIPFR, EIGRP,

VLANs, ACL's, RIPv2 and so on. It is vital for you to know these protocols well.

You must be a certified CCNA expert before you can appear for the CCNP certification examination. You must also have at least a year's experience in the networking field if you wish to appear for the CCNP examination. You can look at different careers in the IT industry if you have a CCNA certification, but with a CCNP certification you can improve your chances of being promoted or obtaining the best job in the industry. There are very few individuals who are CCNP certified and because of this, the demand for CCNP certified individuals is increasing.

You must remember that the Cisco products and systems are complex to deal with. Most organizations hire a team of individuals only to take care of these systems and products. Numerous organizations will be willing to hire you if you have a CCNP certification since you will have a good understanding of the products and systems. A CCNP certification will give you an edge over other individuals since you know how to install, organize, function and even troubleshoot a complex Cisco network. It is for this reason that this certification is essential to obtain. The CCNP examination is only a two-hour examination, but it opens a wide range of prospects for you. This is the main difference between the CCNP and CCNA certification. Before you appear for the CCNP certification, you must ensure that you have a CCNA certification.

Chapter 2

Products and Services Offered by Cisco Networking Solutions

Networking

Cisco gives every company numerous choices for its networking needs. Some of these choices have been listed in the section below. Cisco designed the products mentioned below to meet the changing needs of companies and to improve data storage, access points and servers that are used in the organization.

Networking

Any organization can be certain of the smooth flow of information and smooth business transactions if the network in the company is maintained well. There are numerous networking options that an organization can choose from. These options allow an organization not only to automate the network, but to also decrease the cost of a Wide Area Network thereby improving the business' ability to scale. These networking options also ensure that the network performs very well. These networks are built with enough detail so that it can help it to detect any imminent threat and protect the organization from any damages.

VPN Security Clients

A threat can occur through numerous attack vectors, and it is for this reason that every company must identify a way to secure active protection and connectivity for every endpoint in the network. On average when others can detect threats in 100 days, Cisco can provide such details on threats in just 4.6 hours and process about 1.5 million malware per day.

Switching

It is important to find the right switch for your company. Data is extremely critical for the company in today's world. It is essential to select the right switch to avoid threats faced by the company - now and also in the future. Companies can always use Cisco products to simplify and manage their requirements for IoT, cloud, data center and mobility.

Routing

Cisco's routing product, another networking product can only be used for LAN, WAN, and cloud. It includes integrated security, application optimization, automated provisioning and advanced analytics that deliver a complete and proven solution to your organizational requirements. A company can now automate all of its processes using these routers. These routers also offer application and intelligent path selection, which needs minimal control through customization and programming. A high performing router will always streamline any networking operation thereby reducing the cost, increasing the speed and the deployment of network more agile. Regardless of whether the business is large or small, the Cisco Networking solutions will offer a wide range of products and services that can fit any business model.

Wireless

In today's digital world, one can access any network through a wireless mode. It is imperative that every business have a wireless network since without that, it is hard for a business to communicate with its customers. It is also hard for an employee to work. If a business does not have the right network, its data is privy to attackers. By using Cisco Wireless Enterprise Technology and Mobility products, you can be assured of getting the state-of-the-art access points and top of the line WAN and LAN connections. Cisco offers some of the best products and services in this area and these products are designed to provide high-end security and performance. The best part of it all is that these can fit any small and medium-sized enterprises to large-scale businesses.

Wireless Controllers

As the world is geared up to go wireless, Cisco developed the Wireless Controllers to provide networking options that are secure. These networking options also allow the network to be segmented thereby decreasing the number of threats. They are easy to access and can be enabled even on the cloud. A wireless controller was designed by Cisco to provide faster insights, troubleshoot any problems quickly and deliver a personalized business. These are also designed to have easy upgrading without any interruptions.

Conferencing

Conferencing tools such as WebEx are an open platform that allows companies to integrate features into their unique workflow. This allows the team to collaborate, communicate and work together. This tool connects employees from various countries and provides end-to-end data encryption and protection to keep your work safe. Cisco helps companies to work seamlessly so that the team can meet, share and create.

Unified Communications

People around the globe work together using many collaboration tools. For example IP Telephones for Voice Calling, web and video conferencing, voicemail, mobility desktop sharing, instant messaging, etc. Through Unified Communication Solutions, companies get an option to integrate all their tools and for a seamless user experience, which helps people to work together more effectively. These tools bring real-time communication to companies from anywhere. Services like conferencing, messaging and chat options are a few of the many everyday business applications. Unified Communications offer on-premise, partner-hosted solutions or as a service which is called UC SaaS from the cloud provider.

Advanced Malware Protection

This allows companies to get advanced sandboxing, real-time malware blocking and global threat intelligence to protect from breaches. Since companies cannot prevent threats alone, Cisco ensures analyzing every file, quickly detecting, containing and removing any possible threats to the system.

Web Security

On every legitimate website, there are advanced threats hiding in plain sight in the form of enticing pop-up ads. The employees or clients may put an organization in trouble by clicking on such ads, which can cause extreme damage to the company's data. WSA Web Security Appliances, powered by Cisco Talos protects you by automatically blocking risky sites.

Access Points

The need for security has increased since the growth of mobility and IoT devices. The Cisco Catalyst 910 access point exceeds the new W1-Fi 6 wireless standards and provides radio frequency excellence to high–density environments. These access points help to increase productivity of employees since they allow data to be transmitted at a high speed. This efficient data transmission will help businesses upgrade to new technologies in no time.

Business Collaborations (Collaboration Endpoints)

Cisco is known as the pioneer in technology, which helps to connect businesses across the world through technology. Cisco has over time built several technological solutions that can help a team to come together and work toward a common goal - for individual employees to be able to talk to their peers with less effort. These products include Cisco WebEx Board, Cisco Headset 500 Series, and Cisco WebEx Room Series. Choose the product that suits your company needs, and you are good to go.

Interfaces and Modules

Cisco uses numerous modules and interfaces to deploy advanced networking capabilities. These help every business deliver a new service that will lower the cost to the company.

Networking Management

Cisco uses leading products and services to reduce downtime and improve operational efficiency in businesses. Its products and services also manage the network of the enterprise. These products and services have been designed to fit an organization of any size and also provide access to numerous digital systems and processes. Through these products and services, Cisco provides opportunities to automate policy-based application profiles, which allow the IT team to respond quickly to new business opportunities.

Security

The world is now data driven and the safety of consumer's data has become the topmost priority. Cisco provides solutions that can change the face of data protection. One of the most significant security issues being faced by many companies is that of a cyber threat, which is becoming much smarter and more dangerous. With Cisco's integrated portfolio and industry threat intelligence, you get the scope, scale and capability to keep up with the complexity of every kind of threat.

Advanced Email Security Protection

The primary avenue for attackers is to rely on email to distribute spam, malware, and other threats. To protect from such threats, it is essential to have a strong and powerful email security solution. Through Cisco email security defense against phishing, business email compromising and ransomware, companies can get updates on the security every three to five minutes through Cisco Talos. This Advanced Malware Protection protects against stealthy malware attachments and industry-leading URL intelligence malicious links. It is not only essential to keep the incoming emails safe but also the outgoing mails. Cisco email security has robust data loss-prevention and content-encryption to safeguard sensitive information, which helps you comply with government and industry regulations.

Outdoor and Industrial Access

An outdoor and industrial access product will allow you not only to access data anywhere but also access WiFi outdoors. It also helps people stay connected in numerous locations, which makes it easy for companies to continue their operations with ease. Since these access points are resistant to both extreme cold and heat, it makes it easier for businesses to transmit data through these access points.

Customer Collaborations

A consumer can acquire almost anything in today's digital world. With this comes the need for an organization to respond to all its customers' queries and issues and also provide them with a few personalized services. The mantra 'one size fits all' does not hold up in today's world, and it is for this reason that there are no contact centers any longer. Organizations now try to provide their customers with the right care, and this is no longer an exception but a rule. Cisco has developed products such as Cisco Packaged Contact

Center Enterprise and Cisco Unified Contact Express to enable ease of service.

Product by Company Type

There are numerous medium-sized companies and new businesses that have been set up in the US in the recent past. One of the aims of Cisco is to empower these firms to do better in the market. This goes to show that that the concept of 'one estimate doesn't fit all' works perfectly for Cisco. It is for this reason that Cisco has produced some items as per wants of the organization, hence allowing organizations to work on personalizing their operations, and help them stand out when compared to the other companies.

Services

Apart from the numerous products listed above, Cisco also provides companies, big or small, with the services necessary to install necessary hardware and software and also to train their employees to maintain those installed software. Cisco also works as an advisor and helps organizations and companies implement some IT solutions in their firm. It also helps a company optimize the performance of the company, which improves both efficiency and productivity. Cisco also works on managing the assets of the company. It also takes care of the cloud services. Cisco also sends professionals to train employees to learn more about the digital shift in the market, and also provides the necessary assistance that will help in the growth of the company.

Chapter 3

About CCNA Examination

CCNA or Cisco Certified Network Associate is the wide scope of technical specialties offered to the IT world by Cisco. These industry standard certifications are always supported by the IT industry since they show an individual's specific insight and competency.

There are two section level accreditations that are offered by Cisco: the Cisco Certified Entry Level Technician (CCENT) and the Cisco Certified Technician (CCT) certification. The former certification is for those individuals who are system experts. This accreditation will help these individuals confirm to organizations that they have the necessary skills to operate network support stations. If these individuals have the CTT accreditation they can let organizations know that they can analyze, fix and oversee online essential Cisco networking components.

The Cisco Certified Technician (CTT) gives individuals the chance to specialize in three areas: CCT TelePresence, Data Center or Routing and Switching. The CTT Routing and Switching certification is one of the most sought after certifications since this focuses on the aptitudes required for on-location support and upkeep of Cisco-brand equipment and systems. This certification also gives experts the ability to work with different Cisco routers, switches, connected adornments and cabling. All of these certifications help specialists begin their careers as network experts. They additionally have the essential qualification necessary to opt for a CCNA certification.

Any individual can obtain an associate-level qualification in video, voice, industrial, cloud, wireless, server provider, data center, routing and switching. For instance, numerous organizations are utilizing cloud-based innovation to enable them to stay dexterous and adaptable. The CCNA Cloud Certification is a program that was only intended for system directors and specialists, as they can extend their aptitudes and build on the information that they obtain. The

CCNA Security certification sheds some light on numerous security aspects, which are important for any system security expert to know. Passing the test implies that IT work competitors have what is required to perceive dangers, limit organizational vulnerabilities and oversee complex security frameworks.

The CCNA Routing and Switching examination is one of the most well-known associate level programs offered by Cisco. The requirement for qualifying as a system expert increases since the systems continue to evolve. It is important for some individuals to learn more about how they can design, create and troubleshoot any network issues that may arise.

The systems administration networks always plan video administrations, voice interchanges, and joint effort conditions. The different concepts and ideas covered in the CCNA Routing and Switching examination are significant and can be applied across different modules. The modules that you will need to prepare for while studying for the CCNA Routing and Switching Certification are in line with the appointed assignments of systems administration experts. This program also helps you understand how you can plan and design a system. This also offers help as specialized masters.

When you clear the CCNA Routing and Switching certification, you will have a range of abilities and have amassed a lot of knowledge. As a CCNA associate, you should be able to:

- Explain how a computer network works and how it cooperates with other networked devices.

- Identify network security dangers and depict risk alleviation strategies and countermeasures.

- Arrange, check and investigate a switch with VLAN and communications.

- Understand how various system topologies interface to shape a protected IT arrangement.

- Arrange, confirm and investigate routing and router activities on current Cisco gadgets.

- Actualize an IP addressing scheme and IP Services to meet specific system prerequisites.

- Setup and check WAN connections and execute the best possible strategies for associating with a WLAN Administration.

- Depict and play out the fitting assignments for the Wireless Local Area Network (WLAN) administration.

- Actualize and encouraging Network Address Translation (NAT) and Access Control Lists (ACLs) in branch office systems

Chapter 4

Different Types of CCNA Exam

A n individual can pass numerous associate level examinations to be certified as an expert in that field. These exams all form the foundation for any networking certification.

CCNA Routing and Switching

This section will shed some light on the different certifications that you can obtain within the Routing and Switching area of study. You will also learn more about the significance of these certifications and the exams you will need to appear for to obtain those certifications.

CCNA Cloud

There are numerous organizations that are now welcoming the use of Cloud with open arms. It enables them to convey their business results in a manner that is progressive, coordinated, finely attuned and compelling. Numerous businesses currently use the SaaS model, but as of 2018, over 78% of all the work was being handled on the Cloud.

The CCNA Cloud certification is a job-oriented training program that will help Cloud engineers, administrators and network engineers to not only hone and develop their cloud skillset but also allows them to support their IT department to meet their ever-changing business and technological need.

If you have this certification, you can learn more about how you can execute the basic support and also facilitate the functions on the cloud. You can learn all this from the only organization that provides the complete Cloud and Intercloud story.

You must take the following examinations to receive this certification.

210-451 CLDFND

This test examines your learning of Cisco Cloud Networks, where you will be tested for your understanding of the DC essentials, basics of UF, UC, Storage, Network Services and Virtualization, Windows Server, Hypervisors, Linux OS; remote connectivity/VPN solutions and documentation of design, the framework fabrications, setups and support strategies.

210-455 CLDADM

This examination will test your knowledge and skills regarding the basics of the Cisco Cloud organization along with Cloud provisioning, remediation, monitoring, reporting, the charge-back formats, and the management.

- The portrayal of detail reporting and charge-back.

- Understanding the basics of Cloud framework administration.

- Providing Cloud based on pre-designed templates.

- Distinguishing the different features of the Cisco Cloud management software solution.

- Perform Cloud management, checking and remediation

CCNA Collaboration

This is designed for network engineers, IP network engineers, collaboration engineers and IP telephony engineers who wish to learn and improve their skills of collaboration and video engineering per the voice, data, and other versatile applications. The Cisco CCNA Collaboration certification is a job-oriented training and certification program. The course material provided for this examination will help you improve your understanding and skills, and also improve your value as a professional. It does this by providing you with the necessary skills and aptitude to help IT organizations fulfill their ever-increasing business needs due to the rapid changes in technology. You must clear the 210-060 CICD examination to obtain this certification.

This exam is designed to test your knowledge about the Cisco Unified Communications solutions. You will be tested on your knowledge of final-user and management interfaces, features of telephony and mobility along with the maintenance of UC solutions.

210-065 CIVND

This examination has been designed to test your knowledge and skills, which are essential to implement numerous Cisco Video endpoints that can be found in the United Cisco video frameworks. It will also check your aptitude to execute and resolve Cisco Unified Communication and Collaboration, Digital Media Player and TelePresence in various Cisco business solution models.

CCNA Cyber Ops

Every organization in today's digital world is challenged with identifying breaches in security quickly. It will also need to know how it must react against any imminent threat to the information or data stored in the organization. All the personnel working in Security Operations Centers (SOC's) vigilantly monitor the security frameworks and protect the organizations by swiftly spotting and retaliating against any cyber security threats or potential breaches. The CCNA Cyber Ops accreditation will help you learn more about the skills required for you to work as an associate-level cyber security analysts in the SOCs. From July 2018, The United States Department of Defense (DoD) has affirmed the Cisco CCNA Cyber Ops Certification for the DoD 8570.01-M for the CSSP Analyst and CCSP Incident Responder groups.

You must take the following examinations to receive this certification.

210-250 SECFND

This examination is one of the two that you are required to pass if you wish to obtain a CCNA Cyber Ops certification. You can secure a job as a Security Operations Center (SOC) analyst if you clear this examination. The SECFND examination will test your knowledge and skills in cyber security's primary principles. It will also test the fundamental skills essential to understand the more progressive associate-level course materials required for the second prerequisite exam, 'Implementing Cisco Cyber Security Operations (SECOPS)'.

210-255 SECOPS

If you want to obtain the associate-level certification in CCNA Cyber Ops, you will need to clear this examination. This examination will help you learn more about the skills you will need to develop as an associate-level Security Operations Center (SOC) Security Analyst. This exam tests the knowledge and aptitude required for efficiently handling the different duties and obligations of an associate-level Security Analyst working in a Security Operations Center (SOC).

CCNA Data Center

A data center is deemed to be effective based on its quickness and dexterity. Every data center has been designed for the quick execution of numerous applications, and the quickness is reinforced by an exceptionally versatile framework. A data center has become the primary focus of organizations that are competing in today's digitized world. CCNA Data Center Certification will give you the assurance and agility that is necessary for installing, configuring and maintaining the technology of a data center. This certification will also help you learn more about the concepts of data center infrastructure, networking and technologies, storage networking and unified computing, network virtualization, data center automation and orchestration, and Cisco Application Centric Infrastructure (ACI).

You must take the following examinations to receive this certification.

200-150 DCICN

This exam will test your knowledge about the physical infrastructure, networking, and storage networking concepts of the data center.

200-155 DCICT

This examination will test your knowledge and skills about the physical infrastructure, networking concepts, automation, and storage networking concepts related to a data center.

CCNA Industrial

The Cisco Certified Network Associate Industrial (CCNA Industrial) Certification is designed for plant administrators, traditional network engineers and control system engineers dealing with process control, assembling, and oil/gas ventures, who will be working along with industrial and IT networks. When you clear this certification, you will learn the different skills that are necessary for you to know to design, implement and troubleshoot any issues that arise within a network. It will also provide information on how you can do this while using the best practices necessary for the connected networks present today.

This module consolidates both the theoretical and practical knowledge through some practical lab work and exercises. This module will help you develop the skills necessary for working in the IT industry and also enhance your knowledge about the current infrastructures that different organizations incorporate in their functions. It will also provide information about the infrastructure that will support the future results of the business.

The prerequisites for this certification are Industrial Networking Specialist or CCENT or CCNA Routing and Switching or any other CCIE certification.

200 -601 IMINS2

This examination will test your understanding and knowledge about the concepts and technology that you can find in an automated manufacturing environment. This exam will cover the Common Industrial Protocol (CIP) and ProfiNET industrial conventions. It will also test you on the fundamental design of the support network infrastructure to optimize the effectiveness of the Industrial Ethernet.

CCNA Security

The CCNA Security certification will help an individual garner the skills and knowledge that they will need to work as associate level representatives in the IT department of any organization. If you have this certification, you will be hired as a network professional since you will have the abilities required to develop a security infrastructure, perceive dangers and vulnerabilities to networks and alleviate any security breaches. The CCNA Security educational program emphasizes primary security technologies. It also provides information about the establishment, investigation and vigilance of network instruments for maintaining the virtues; discretion and the accessibility of information and instruments, as well as their competency of all the innovations that use Cisco security structure.

210-260 IINS

The CCNA Security examination will test your knowledge about the different aspects of security including security network infrastructure, your understanding of the fundamental concepts of security, verification of secure access, VPN encryption, firewalls, prevention of any breach and the endpoint security while using SIEM technology, Cloud and Virtual Network topology, BYOD, Identity Service Engine (ISE), 801.1 x Authentication and a other cyber-security related concepts.

This examination will help you validate your skills of designing, installing, monitoring and troubleshooting any secure network which will help the service provider secure the data and also allow the data to be accessible to the devices connected to the network.

CCNA Service Provider

The Cisco Certified Network Associate Service Provider (CCNA SP) certification was designed for those individuals who work as network engineers, specialists, and planners for any service provider. Their primary focus is on the recent developments, technology, and trends within the Service Provider industry's fundamental networking, and the examination covers these aspects.

You must take the following examinations to receive this certification.

640-875 SPNGN1

This examination will test your basic knowledge and the basic skills needed to support the network of any service provider. To learn more about the exam, please refer to the following link: https://www.cisco.com/c/en/us/training-events/training-certifications/exams/current-list/spngn1.html

640-878 SPNGN2

This exam will test your aptitude and knowledge that is important for you to know if you are going to execute, maintain and support the network of any service provider. An applicant must get ready for this examination by taking up the Building Cisco Service Provider Next-Generation Networks, Part 2 (SPNGN2) course.

CCNA Wireless

Cisco has a wireless innovation department that has been placing a lot of demands on the network. These demands in turn affect the individuals working on networks. Every organization will require a set of professionals who can work on the network and ensure that the network has been configured properly. These individuals must also monitor the network and troubleshoot if necessary. You can improve your skills and enhance your knowledge of these networks when you prepare for the CCNA wireless certification.

Prerequisites for this certification are Cisco CCENT, CCNA Routing and Switching or any other CCIE certification.

You must take the following examinations to receive this certification.

200-355 WIFUND

This examination will test your knowledge about how to install, configure and troubleshoot a small sized network or a Wide Area Network.

The next few chapters will shed some light on the CCNA Routing and Switching examination.

Chapter 5

About CCNA Routing and Switching

Called the holy grail of Cisco Certifications, the CCIE was one of the most difficult certifications to achieve and must be achieved before moving on to other networking courses. This overwhelming approach of winning or losing at the test made it impossible to succeed and, in turn, predictably did not work out for most individuals. Due to this, Cisco responded to the issue by creating a series of new certifications, which made it easier to achieve the CCIE prize. It gave the employers an approach that could accurately measure and rate the skills of a prospect and a current employee of the organization. This dynamic paradigm shift in Cisco Certification truly opened doors through which only very few were permitted.

From the year 1998, the CCNA Cisco Certified Network Associate Certification became the first milestone certification of its kind. It also became the official prerequisite to meet the propelled levels of the certification, which were then changed in the year **2007** when Cisco declared the Cisco Certified Entry Networks Technicians (CCENT) Certification in March. Cisco announced the updates to the CCENT and CCNA Routing and Switching tests on their website.

The Cisco Routing and Switching was the most prominent certification by a long shot and would have remained this way. However, the Data Center Certification turned out to be winner as organizations moved to data-focused technologies. The track record likewise gives a decent show with regards to the circumstances. Understanding the establishment of Routing and Switching before attempting another certification track is something I would like to suggest. All things being considered, you need your CCENT certification to begin progress.

As organizations embrace programmable network architectures, the skill set expected of center network engineers is developing. CLI-based interactions with routing and switching frameworks are offering an approach to controller-based interactions driven by business and application approaches. To satisfy this need, Cisco has refreshed its generally mainstream certification, CCNA Routing, and Switching, to enable IT professionals to completely saddle the intensity of the most recent Cisco technologies. The entrants who let their CCNA Routing and Switching Certification slip by will need to focus on these changes. The CCNA Routing and Switching Certification has been refreshed to meet these most recent changes in technologies:

- Awareness of programmable network (SDN) architectures and the partition of control plane and information plane.

- Expanded VPN subjects to incorporate DMVPN, site-to-site VPN and customer VPN technologies.

- Increased spotlight on IPv6 routing protocols, configuration, and knowledge

- Understanding of cloud assets conveyed in enterprise network architectures

- Knowledge of QoS concepts, including checking, forming and policing mechanisms to manage congestion of various types of traffic.

Once you obtain the CCNA Routing and Switching Certification, you can show your present and future employers and managers that you have the necessary skills to excel in the industry. That being said, you will need to stay abreast of any changes or developments being made in this field to ensure that you stand out and have an edge over your competitors.

One of the prime reasons certification holders let their credentials lapse is because they have held a position where they never again require a present certification. But with technology changing so quickly, this may be the perfect time to reexamine their skillsets and upgrade them from time to time.

Before getting certified for CCNA Routing and Switching, it is important to pass the entry-level examination. After this, there are two more divisions and after passing them you will get certified as a CCNA Routing and Switching Associate.

The CCENT Examination

This may be an entry-level examination that every candidate needs to clear, but do not make the mistake of thinking that this is an easy exam. Perhaps the entry level for Cisco's certification is partially simple, yet it is not for somebody with no experience attempting to break into the exceedingly rewarding yet testing IT field. Most amateurs look at obtaining the Comp TIA A+ and Network+ certifications. This is a good thing to do since you can develop a foundation that will help you when you write your CCNA Routing and Switching examination (this is only true for the new CCNA exam which was developed in the year 2013). You should remember that the exam is hard, and if you do not prepare well for the examination, you will certainly find it difficult to answer questions during the test. You must remember that the newer versions of the examination are harder than the old CCNA examinations. You will understand this more when you begin to study for the examination. Once you obtain the certificate, you can be certain that employers will want to hire you. This certificate will also help you move ahead in your career in the networking industry. Therefore, you must work hard and study as much as you can before you pay for the examination. This means that you need to perform adequate research to understand if this is the certification you need and if you can spend sufficient amount of time to prepare for this exam. You must remember that the exams are expensive, and therefore you should make an informed decision.

Cisco Certified Network Associate - Routing and Switching (CCNA Routing and Switching)

Once you obtain the CCENT certification, you can appear for the ICND1 and ICND2 examinations to obtain your CCNA Routing and Switching certification. This is one of the most sought-after certifications in the networking industry. The CCENT examination costs $150, and you cannot pass this examination by reading some material.

These exams are difficult and the questions asked are often tricky to solve. Therefore, you will need to cover different material and scour through exam dumps to test your level of understanding. It is always a good idea to sign up for an online tutorial class since the tutors will help you understand how you should study for and clear the examination. Once you obtain this certification, you can obtain the CCNP (Cisco Certified Networking Professional) certification.

If you choose to take the CCNA Routing and Switching examination, you can land the job you really want. You may not be willing to take two examinations to obtain the certificate. In this instance, you can choose to take the composite examination. It is important to remember that the syllabus covered in this examination is extensive, which means that you will need to spend a good amount of time in studying for this examination. Regardless of whether you choose to take one exam or two, you must ensure that you have some practical knowledge. This means that you should take as many labs as you can. Additionally, you should focus on taking practice exams and looking at exam dumps to familiarize yourself with the different questions that can be asked in the examination.

Why do you need to become a CCENT and CCNA Routing and Switching Certified?

Cisco has designed the CCNA Routing and Switching Certification to enable an employer to learn more about the aptitude of their employees. An employer can use this certification to verify if the employee meets the criteria for some roles. Therefore, if you are looking for an employee w

Cisco designed the CCNA Routing and Switching Certification to help employers gauge their prospective employees' aptitude. These employers can also use this certification to understand if an employee meets some of the necessary criteria for a role. Therefore, if you are someone who is in the networking industry or wants to change roles, you should take the CCNA Routing and Switching examination since that will help you establish a sustainable career.

This examination will not only help you understand the Cisco Internetwork Operating System (IOS) and Cisco hardware, but also understand how the Internet works. There are some companies that hire employees as network engineers simply because they are certified. Therefore, if you choose to take this examination, and manage to clear it in the first attempt you can land a job in any networking company.

What are the skills required to become CCENT and CCNA Routing and Switching certified?

The ICND1 examination will test your knowledge and skills with respect to small networks. This examination will test you on the installation of the network, how the network works and what you will need to do to overcome issues. You will also learn more about LAN switching technologies, IP services network device security, IP routing technologies, network device security, troubleshooting and the IPv6 protocol. The ICND2 examination will test your skills and your understanding on how to install, work with and troubleshoot larger networks. The test will check your understanding of IP routing technologies, LAN switching technologies, IP services (syslog, FHRP, and SNMP v2 and v3), troubleshooting and WAN technologies.

What does it take to become certified in CCNA Routing and Switching

If you want to obtain the CCNA Routing and Switching Certification, you must take the Composite examination. This is a combined examination that is slightly difficult to clear. The syllabus covered in this examination is vast, and it is impossible to understand every concept and remember them so you can answer the required number of questions to pass the examination. The different topics that are covered in the CCNA Composite examination have been taken from the ICND1 and ICND2 examinations.

If you do not wish to appear for the composite examination, you can appear for the ICND1 and ICND2 examinations. You must always think carefully and plan your study route before you sign up for the examination. You can choose to give one examination instead of two, and there is a high probability of clearing the examination if you study for the required time. Remember that you must practice and work hard. You will need to clear the following papers if you choose to take up two examinations instead of one:

1. Exam: Interconnecting Cisco Networking Devices Part 1 (ICND1)

2. Exam: Interconnecting Cisco Networking Devices Part 2 (ICND2)

Where Do You Take your Exam?

You are required to register for the exam on Pearson VUE regardless of whether you choose to take the ICND1 and ICND2 examinations or the composite examination. If you want to gather some more information about these examinations, please visit the website using the following link: www.vue.com.

Follow the steps given below if you have decided to clear the examination:

1. The first thing you must do is choose the exam that you want to appear for. If you want to take up the composite examination, you should choose the code 200-125. If you want to sign up for the ICND1 and ICND2 examinations, you should choose the codes 100-105 and 200-105.

2. After you have selected the examination that you want to appear form you will need to visit the nearest examination center and register for that exam. Remember that you will need to pay for the exam in advance, and you can sit for the exam within a year after you have made the payment.

3. You can sit for the exam when you decide to take the exam or give yourself a six week deadline before you sit for the exam. That being said, if you cannot appear for the exam on the day you have decided to sit for it, you must wait for five days before you sign up again for the exam. In the event that you know that you will be unable to sit for the exam, you should send Pearson VUE an email at least twenty-four hours before the examination. They will help you reschedule the examination at no extra cost.

4. Once you schedule the examination, Pearson VUE will send all the instructions to you via email, and will also provide some information about what you will need to do at the examination center. You will also be given information about the different items you will need to carry with you to the center.

5. It is important that you always carry an original copy of the document or identification proof.

Always Use the Material Provided by Cisco Authorized Publishers

You must always purchase the course material from a well-known publisher. The best option would be to purchase this material from a publisher who has been authorized by Cisco. When you do this, you do not have to worry about having to look for new study material since the material that you will be purchasing will cover all the information that you will need to know for the examination. It is also a good idea to sign up for a course that is led by an instructor, as the trainer will guide you on how you should prepare for the examination. The trainer will also shed some light on the different material that you can study from, and also provide you with some links that you can use.

Chapter 6

Why Should You Appear For the CCNA Routing and Switching Examination

❧————————❧

Are you aware of the importance of obtaining a Cisco certification? If you are armed with a Cisco certification, it will open up various career opportunities for you and create a strong technical foundation. It offers validation of all the skills that are essential for moving ahead in this tech-oriented world. It will bring in quantifiable results while working as a networking professional. There are multiple benefits of getting a CCNA Certification. As a Network Administrator and Network Engineer, your responsibilities are continually increasing with each passing day and obtaining a certification in CCNA can elevate your status in the organization and may also help you attain a pay raise.

One of the best ways to prepare for a successful career in networking is to obtain the CCNA Routing and Switching Certification. This by itself is a great reason to obtain the certification. There are, however, many more reasons. This chapter lists the many advantages of obtaining a CCNA Routing and Switching certification.

Certification is the Foundation That Networking Careers Are Built Upon

Many network engineers and networking employees have been trying their best to obtain CCNA certifications ever since CCNA started its different programs and certifications. Studies conducted by IDC state that many networking companies look for different Cisco skills when they are hiring employees. Most employees include Cisco skills when compared to every other skill. It has always been important for employees to have a good understanding of different network protocols and network infrastructure. It is also important to learn how these work together. The need for this is now intensifying. If you obtain a CCNA Routing and Switching Certification, you can obtain the knowledge and expertise required to succeed in the networking industry. This knowledge will also help you troubleshoot any issues that occur within the network.

Certification Gives You a Full Range of Training Options

You can learn in more than one way. There are many Authorized Learning Partners, and each of these partners offer numerous training options that make it easier for anybody to earn their Routing and Switching certification. You can choose to enroll in a virtual classroom, an instructor-led training or hands-on labs for both the ICND1 and ICND2 components of the examination. The Cisco Learning Network Store also offers learning labs, self-paced e-learning and practice exams that will help you prepare well for the certification. Additionally, Cisco Press, which is an authorized publisher, offers a lot of resources that you can use to prepare for the examination. Another wonderful aspect of CCNA certifications is that they give you the opportunity to study and prepare for the exams according to your convenience. You can either opt for a self-paced curriculum or enroll yourself for the training program Cisco offers. You will learn more about this in the coming chapters.

Certification Gives You More Career Options

Since the CCNA Certification was started, Cisco Certifications have been warranted by network engineers and organizations alike across the globe. As indicated by an ongoing report from the IDC (International Data Corporation), Cisco abilities are among the most wanted for aptitudes while enlisting potential candidates. This need is increasing by the day. A Cisco CCNA Routing and Switching accreditation will validate your knowledge and expertise about data and ability in networking. When you take up CCNA certification and successfully clear it, you can place yourself as a network administrator capable of troubleshooting network problems prevalent in networking areas and will be able to create the infrastructure to back it.

Once you are the proud holder of CCNA Certification, you will have an edge over others in your field. It can give you better recognition when you are handing out your resumes for any job openings in the field of Cisco networking operations. The three-year validity of this certification will ensure that you have the time to make the most of all the knowledge and skills you have acquired during the certification program.

You will have many career opportunities if you obtain the CCNA Routing and Switching Certification. Based on a survey conducted by IDC, it was identified that seven out of ten organizations look for certifications when they are promoting or hiring an individual. You can progress to the expert levels in the routing and switching track using the different courses provided by Cisco. You can also use the skills you develop as a routing and switching expert in technologies like Collaboration, Cloud, Network Programmability, Data Center, Security or Wireless. These areas are developing and are propelling the IT industry forward. If you have a certification in routing and switching, you can change the direction of your career at any point.

Certification Keeps You Current on All the Latest Technology Changes

In addition to bringing about major network architecture changes, for instance, the Cisco DNA, Cisco continuously works on creating IT landscapes conducive to various technological developments that will have an impact on your job profile as a networking professional. Cisco always ensures that it is aware of all the changes that are taking place in technology and the IT industry. It does this to ensure that students are aware of how the changes in technology will affect the certification or their role in a company. The CCNA Routing and Switching exam is not an exception to this. Cisco constantly revises the curriculum to ensure that students are aware of every small change made in the industry. The latest curriculum will give you an understanding of QoS (Quality of Service) elements and how they are used, the network functions and interactions of firewalls and wireless access points and controllers, along with a renewed focus on IPv6 and basic network security. So, all this means that you will be able to keep up with the technological advancements taking place in your organization and industry.

Learning Curve

In your pursuit of acquiring the CCNA Certifications, you will be able to improve your knowledge and create the foundations for an efficient way of understanding the different fundamental aspects of Cisco networking. Regardless of whether you have years of experience under your belt in the field of networking or not, you will certainly need to keep up with the growing demand for specialized skills to keep up with your competition. The age-old saying, "nothing can substitute experience," stands corrected when it comes to keeping up with all the innovations and technologies of the digitized world that we live in. It is essential that you keep yourself updated with all the recent technological developments taking place in the IT field.

Before you can think about completing the whole Cisco program, there is a prerequisite that you must fulfill. A lot of Cisco certifications demand that you successfully pass the CCNA exam before you are eligible for anything else. So, the CCNA certification is like the stepping-stone to move ahead in the Cisco Training courses.

Certification Helps You Learn from Your Peers

Many individuals and professionals are gearing up to prepare for different Cisco certifications. It is for this reason that Cisco has developed the Cisco Learning Network, which is a learning and career development community. There are a million professionals in this community. This community provides valuable support and also helps the members learn, study and prepare for the certification examinations. When you are a member of the Cisco Learning Network, you will gain access to training videos, study groups, a wealth of examination information and peer-to-peer advice.

You'll Be Certified by the Networking Leader

Cisco was one of the first companies to introduce routing and switching, and it continues to lead the way. It has the largest market share, and most of its products are used by companies across different industries. Overwhelming Internet traffic moves on the different network pathways that are built using the Cisco infrastructure products. If you know how to work on Cisco products and have certifications to back it up, your skills will certainly be more marketable, and you will be in demand.

Certification Helps Increase Your Paycheck

Since there is a shortage of talent in the networking industry, the salaries for a networking employee are usually high. If you have a Cisco certification in routing and switching, you can increase your salary. As per a report by Robert Half Technology, in the 2018 Technology Salary Guide, CCNA routing and switching certification is one the most sought after certifications in the industry. This guide also stated that some employers were willing to increase the salaries by five or ten percent if the candidates meet all criterions. Many organizations also offer their employees monetary rewards for obtaining a Cisco certification.

If you are the holder of CCNA certification, then it means you will be able to look out for better career opportunities. Additionally, these qualifications also give you the chances to ask for a salary hike. The employees in an IT team are given their roles based on all the certifications they hold. So, having a CCNA certification will give you the potential advantage of quickly climbing up the corporate ladder. If your appraisal is right around the corner, then this certification can also help you grab a quick salary hike.

Don't Forget: There Is Value in Recertification

The Routing and Switching Certification is only valid for three years. That being said, you can always recertify yourself. The certificate is only valid for three years since Cisco monitors the industry and does its best to ensure that the certifications it provides always keep pace with the requirements of the IT industry. When you are willing to learn constantly and are happy to recertify yourself, you can ensure that you are aware of every new development made in the industry. You will learn more about the recertification policy of Cisco in the coming chapters.

Certification Prepares You for Network Evolution in the Digital Era

Now that businesses are being transformed through digitization, there is a radical change in network infrastructure. Many manual processes have been replaced with the software-driven network architecture that depends on analytics, automation, visualization, cloud service management and whether the network is open and extensible. IDC revealed that a recent study concluded that the most important roles in the IT industry are network engineers and network architects. A professional who wants to improve his standing in the IT industry should embrace this shift.

Secure Your Career through Routing and Switching

It is important to remember that digital transformation is changing the face of the world. This is especially true in case of the business world since every company should take advantage of the different technology to maintain a competitive edge. In today's world, every business initiative is a technology initiative, and an IT professional is expected not only to stay on top of technology, but also improve different processes and the business.

Businesses now move forward because of the Internet of Things (IoT), which is constantly evolving. The importance of technology like mobility, big data, security, network design, cloud, application development, data center operations, systems or services integration, and enterprise architecture is increasing. So, how does this affect you or your career? Since there are many developments taking place in the IT industry, managers now look to hire people with certifications. These certifications will prove that the individual is aware of all the new developments in IT. They also look for people who have experience in the core routing and switching industry. A recent study showed that there was a shortage of employees with critical IT skills. The managers who were a part of this study also said that they were willing to hire candidates or promote employees depending on their certifications. When you obtain a certification that is important to so many companies, you improve your status in the industry.

Globally Accepted

Another brilliant thing about the CCNA Certification is that it is globally recognized and accepted in different countries across the globe. So, the validity of a CCNA certification doesn't have any geographical constraints. All those networking experts armed with CCNA Certifications under their belt are in a better position to negotiate for not just a higher pay scale but also better positions in an organization. At present, the number of CCNA jobs open on the market is steadily increasing, and they all require that the potential candidates have some CCNA certification as one of their criteria for job eligibility. You can use the knowledge that you gain through the CCNA Certification as a stepping stone for learning more about different and newer modules of networking and cyber security courses to boost your career. Attaining the first certification might seem rather complicated and also an uphill battle at times; however, once you take the first step, you will be able to get the hang of things. After all, beginning well is half done, and this stands true for CCNA certification.

Certification Helps You Stand Out with Your Employer

It isn't just you who stands to gain by attaining a CCNA certification. It is beneficial for the organization that you are part of. You can ask any potential employer, and they will tell you that a certified professional is competent to work in the highly competitive world of information technology. Once equipped with this certification, you can prove to your employer that you have the knowledge as well as the essential skills for getting the job done.

Your employer will know that you want to excel in your career when you begin to prepare for the CCNA Routing and Switching examination. A manager will notice that kind of initiative. Based on research conducted by IDC, it can be said that close to eighty-two percent of leaders in digital transformation believe that people who have a certification help to accelerate innovation. There is also some credibility that is associated with a Cisco Certification. Many employers use the CCNA Routing and Switching Certification as a criterion to hire a candidate. In this ever-changing world, it will always do you good to have certain additional skills to cement your stand as an expert in your field.

Unique Way of Learning

The Cisco Learning Network is unique since it is a social network platform that is widely used for learning. This is the future of the Internet, think of it as Internet 2.0. This network offers access to social sharing of information across the globe with various other professionals and students alike. The network also offers a wide array of services like training, simulation labs, corporate internships, job listings, programs for mentorship and recruitment and various other things.

Less-Extensive Outline

Networking professionals always seem to question which of the two is better - Microsoft or Cisco? The Cisco Certification Programs don't include any broad frameworks, which make it simpler for the course-applicant to complete the modules. Since these certifications aren't extremely demanding, you can also pursue any other additional certification that you might want. When you get Cisco CCNA certified, you can progress towards becoming an expert in other areas of certification in the networking domain. Apart from all the quantitative benefits discussed in this chapter, there is another benefit that you will achieve. This benefit isn't quantifiable, and it is personal satisfaction. Once you get certified, you will certainly experience a sense of personal satisfaction, especially if you have meant to undertake a professional certification course. Also, don't you think that you will feel quite proud to add those four magical letters (CNNA) after your name on a business card?

The ever-increasing developments and innovations in the field of networking technologies across the globe foretell an impending shortage of qualified networking professionals. So, what can be a better way to cement your stand as a qualified networking professional than by obtaining CCNA Certification?

The Changing Role of Core Network Engineers

Many enterprises are now adopting programmable network architectures. It is for this reason that employees will need to develop the necessary skills to work with those architectures. Many companies are getting rid of the CLI-based interactions in routing and switching infrastructures and adopting a controller-based interaction that is driven by application and business policies. It is for this reason that Cisco has updated the curriculum for Routing and Switching to ensure that every IT professional is aware of how to use the technology. People who have not renewed their certification must pay attention to the following changes that have been made by Cisco to the Routing and Switching certification:

- Increased focus on IPv6 routing protocols, configuration, and knowledge

- Understanding of cloud resources deployed in enterprise network architectures

- Expanded VPN topics to include DMVPN, site-to-site VPN, and client VPN technologies

- Awareness of programmable network (SDN) architectures and the separation of control plane and data plane

- Knowledge of QoS concepts, including marking, shaping, and policing mechanisms to manage congestion of various types of traffic

As mentioned earlier, Cisco does its best to ensure that it incorporates the new developments in technology in all the certifications that it provides. When you obtain the Routing and Switching Certification, you can prove to organizations and to others in the IT industry that you are aware of the latest solutions that you can use in the industry. Many professionals do not renew their certificate or recertify themselves since they no longer require that certification. This is, however, a bad idea since you may lose out on future opportunities.

Chapter 7

The Simplest Way to Earn the Certification

E verybody in the networking industry is aware that a Cisco certification comes with numerous benefits for both the individual and the organization. If you are looking for a way to boost your career in the IT industry, it is important that you complete at least one Cisco certification. Cisco offers numerous certifications that a novice or an expert can complete to enhance their experience in the IT industry. The different examinations offered by Cisco have been listed in the next few chapters in the book.

Since there are different certifications offered by Cisco, it is always good to know what order you should complete them in. The CCENT certification is an entry-level certification followed by the CCNA certifications. The latter are classified as associate level certifications. The CCIP certifications come next and are followed by the CCNA and CCIE certifications, both of which improve an individual's career.

The objective of a Cisco certification is to help you improve your IT career. This section will provide an insight into what the CCNA Routing and Switching Certification is about, and will help you identify the path you should take to obtain the certification.

Basics of the CCNA Routing and Switching Certification

It is always a good idea to earn the CCNA Routing and Switching Certification since it helps to develop your IT career. Most businesses, big or small, are moving towards a controller-based architecture. This means that it is important for you to improve your networking skills to suit the field. You should also remember that the networking field is volatile. It is true that the skills that you need to develop to work as a core network engineer have changed over the years. Therefore, if you can update your skills faster, you can fit into the role easily. Otherwise, you may miss out on some job opportunities or lose your current job.

The Routing and Switching certification will help you understand the different technologies that you can use in networking. This certification does not come with any necessary prerequisites.

You can obtain the CCNA Routing and Switching Certification either by passing one exam or two exams. This is the choice that Cisco gives you. You can either choose to take the composite 200-125 examination or take the 100-105 ICND1 and 200-105 ICND2 examinations.

About 200-125 CCNA Exam

The 200-125 examination is a composite examination, and it combines the ICND1 and ICND2 courses. Most candidates do choose to take this examination. The test will validate your knowledge and skills regarding LAN Switching technologies, infrastructure services, infrastructure security, infrastructure management, WAN technologies, and other network fundamentals. Like every other Cisco certification examination, you will need to answer seventy questions in ninety minutes. These questions will come in different formats – simulations, multiple choice multiple answers, multiple choice single answers and drag and drops. If you work as a network administrator, network engineer associate, network support engineer, network specialist or network analyst, you should take this examination.

Recommended Training

It is imperative that you take up the Interconnecting Cisco Networking Devices: Accelerated (CCNAX) v3.0 course if you want to ensure that you clear the 200-125 examination, which is the composite CCNA examination. The course has all the information you would need to know to clear the examination. The course will also help you learn more about the topics that are covered in the examination.

As mentioned earlier, you can also take the 100-105 ICND1 and the 200-105 ICND2 examination to obtain the CCNA routing and switching certification.

100-105 ICND1 Examination

This exam is a ninety minute examination. In this examination, you will only be tested through fifty-five questions. The exam will test your skills, expertise and knowledge regarding infrastructure services, network fundamentals, infrastructure maintenance, and LAN switching technologies.

200-105 ICND2 Exam

In this examination, you will be tested on the WAN technologies, LAN switching technologies, infrastructure services, IPv4 and IPv6 routing technologies and maintenance. You have ninety minutes to answer sixty questions. These questions will test both your knowledge and your skills. The format of the questions is the same as those that are featured in the 100-105 examination.

Exam Preparation

Cisco is at the top when compared to different IT vendors. Cisco provides you with the required tools and material that will make it easy for you to earn your certification in the first attempt. Cisco constantly tries to improve the material that it creates for these certification to ensure that it provides readers with the latest information. From the Cisco Learning network to self-study materials as well as some exam dumps, you have different material that you can use to clear your examination. This section lists some of the tools that you can use to prepare for the exam. These tools will help you strengthen your understanding of the numerous concepts you will be learning.

Self-Study Materials

The Cisco Learning network provides numerous self-study material that you can use to obtain your certification. You should always enroll for the different courses available on the learning network like the Interconnecting Cisco Network Devices (parts one and two). You should also look at the labs that are conducted for these courses. The subjects and topics covered in these courses will help you learn all the concepts that you will need to cover in the composite examination. Numerous practice exams are available on the learning network that will help you gauge your knowledge. More information about these courses has been provided later in the book.

Training Videos And Webinars

You can always go through the different learning and training sessions that are provided on the Cisco learning web. These sessions will help you learn more in very little time. There are numerous resources available on the learning network that are covered in detail in this book.

Study Groups

It is always a good idea to join a study group when you decide to appear for the examination since you can ensure that you prepare well for the examination. You can always build your network. This group will also act as a support group since you will be studying with them to cover the different concepts in the syllabus.

Exam Dumps

An exam dump is as important, if not more important, as the study group you want to join or the study material that you want to read. These dumps will always contain all the questions that you can be asked in any certification examination, and it is for this reason that you should always go through the dump when you prepare for the exam. When you have understood the different topics covered in the syllabus, you can practice all the questions in the exam dump to strengthen your understanding. These dumps will also help you familiarize yourself with different questions.

Recertification

The CCNA Routing and Switching Certification has a validity period of three years. That being said, you can always extend the validity by earning a certification that is at a professional or expert level. For instance, you can earn a CCIE certification that is valid for two years. You can easily extend the validity period of the routing and switching certification by obtaining the CCIE certification. You will learn more about how you can recertify yourself later in the book.

In simple words, it is important to remember that you can achieve a lot by earning any CCNA certification. Regardless of what experience you have, you can excel in your profession if you choose to earn different certifications that Cisco provides. You will always find a good job with a good salary if you obtain these certifications.

Chapter 8

Frequently Asked Questions and Myths

FAQ

What changes have been made to the associate-level certification programs offered by Cisco?

Cisco declared on Walk 26, 2013 that it was planning to update or redesign the associate-level certification programs. This includes the CCNA and Cisco CCENT certifications. Cisco works on restructuring these courses to ensure that the course material is aligned with the changes in the technology in the routing and switching industry. The course material for these courses also includes advanced switching and routing technologies including security, remote and voice. This certification was previously called the CCNA Certification, and has now been broken down into multiple segments, and one segment is the routing and switching certification.

Additionally, most associate level examinations including the CCNA Voice, CCNA SP Operations, CCNA Security, and CCNA

Wireless examinations consider the CCENT Certification as a prerequisite. You should visit the Cisco Learning Network t learn more about these associate-level certifications. This network will also help you learn more about the numerous changes that are made to the syllabus.

Are there changes being made to the CCNA Routing and Switching Exam?

Cisco has split the CCNA certification into the ICND1 and ICND2 examinations. Cisco has included the following topics in the syllabus for the certification: IPv6, investigating and the most recent Cisco routing and switching technology and software. Cisco, as mentioned earlier, always includes newer concepts in the syllabus since there are improvements and advancements being made in this industry. The exams 640-816 ICND2, 640-822 and 640-802 will now be replaced by the 200-101 ICND2, 100-101 ICND1 and 200-120 CCNA respectively.

Why have so many new topics been included to the CCNA and CCENT Routing and Switching exams?

Numerous Cisco clients across the globe have affirmed that they require every employee with a Cisco certification, especially a CCNA certification to have better abilities and knowledge. To accommodate this request, Cisco has moved a few subjects from the ICND2 certification to the ICND1 certification examination. If you pass the ICND1 examination now, you will certainly have better skills and more knowledge when compared to a student who passed the previous ICND1 examination. The new syllabus will now help you learn more about the different topics covered in this examination. Ensure that you clear this examination before you appear for the ICND2 examination. It is true that this addition made to the syllabus is slightly difficult for most students to comprehend, but it is always a good idea to clear these examinations if you want to have an edge over your competition.

If I want to obtain the CCNA Routing and Switching Certification, what are the necessary requirements that I need to adhere to?

If you want to obtain the CCNA Routing and Switching Certification, you must clear the following exams:

· 200-125 CCNAX Composite Exam

OR

· 100-105 ICND1

· 200-105 ICND2

Is there a formal training course that I will need to attend to obtain the certification?

There is no necessity to attend any formal training if you want to appear for these examinations. That being said, it is always a good idea for you just take up a few instructor-led sessions while you are preparing for the examination. These sessions will give you the chance to learn more about the subject.

Where should I register to take up an instructor-led training course?

It is imperative to keep in mind that only those Learning Partners who are authorized by Cisco are allowed to provide instructor-led sessions. These sessions will always be given by those instructors who have been certified by Cisco. You should to visit the Learning Partner Locator on the Cisco site to identify the centers that are the closest to you.

Are there any prerequisites that I will need to meet to obtain the CCNA Routing and Switching Certification?

You can take up the exam at any point in time since there are no prerequisites. That being said, it is always good to have some experience in the networking field.

What job roles can I apply for once I obtain the CCNA Routing and Switching Certification?

You will be prepared for the following roles once you obtain the certification:

· Network Support Engineer

· Network Specialist

· Network Administrator

· Network Engineer Associate

· Network Analyst

How soon must I recertify my certification?

It is important to remember that the validity period for the CCNA Routing and Switching examination is only three years, and it is important that you recertify yourself after the period ends. The following chapter provides further information about how you can recertify yourself.

Are there any self-study material that I can use to prepare for the certification?

There is a lot of self-study material that Cisco offers. Some of the options are:

·   Cisco Certification Practice Exams

·   E-learning courses

·   Cisco Press

·   Cisco Learning Labs

Myths about CCNA

An issue with the Internet is that it gives some people the power to spread incorrect information about anything. The Internet also allows rumors and incorrect information to spread quickly. The fact is that the story is always exaggerated as it moves from one platform to the next, and the CCNA examinations are no exception to this. There are a few myths about the CCNA and CCNP examinations, which have been covered in this section.

The questions you are asked in the exam are based on the survey that you fill out at the start of the exam.

Every student is required to complete a survey before he or she begins the test. This survey will ask the candidates about the different topics they are comfortable with and also talks about some technologies that they are comfortable with. It is difficult to rate yourself ISDN, Frame Relay and other technologies since you are about to take an examination that covers those topics. Therefore, it is possible that you may worry about how the questions will impact your examination. The truth is that your answers to the questions in the survey do not matter. There are some forums and posts on the Internet, which will tell you that you must always rate yourself excellent on any topic that is being asked. They believe that the questions asked from that topic will be easy for one to cover. If you lower the rating, the difficulty of the questions asked from that topic will increase. Cisco has debunked this myth, and it is important that you do not read too much into the questions asked in the survey. You should not worry too much when you are filling out the survey.

When you answer a question incorrectly, the exam will ask you questions from that topic until you get one answer right.

Cisco does not follow the pattern of adaptive testing in any of the certification examinations that it conducts. All the questions asked during the examination will be taken from a large question base. If you have appeared for the Novell examination or the GMAT, you will understand what I mean by adaptive testing. Therefore, it goes without saying that the CCNA examinations are not nerve wrecking.

Your answer will be marked wrong for the simulator questions if you include an extra command.

Both the CCNA and CCNP examinations use the simulator engine. This engine will only act like a router or a switch. Therefore, you can use some extra commands during the examination. You will be given instructions and information about the engine that you are using before the exam. Remember to relax and try to configure the switch the same way you did when you were practicing your labs.

You are ready to pass your exam when you walk into the room with a combination of configuration troubleshooting skills, hands-on experience and theoretical knowledge. You should never let some Internet gossip distract you.

Things to Keep in Mind

CCNA is a comprehensive exam.

Regardless of which CCNA certification you are appearing for, you will notice that the questions are spread across the different topics covered in the syllabus. You will see that the questions are not only based on TCP/IP topics but also cover questions on how routing protocols can be used to span trees. There is a lot to cover in the CCNA examination, and it is for this reason that the exam is deemed to be difficult. Instructors and experts state that every candidate should always focus on the ICND subjects if they wish to create a foundation for themselves. This means that you will need to understand everything in the material for those exams.

The CCNA exam is very quick.

The CCNA examination is a very quick examination in the sense that you only have ninety minutes to answer sixty questions. It is very difficult for anybody to answer those many questions in the short time span, but if you are well prepared, you can zoom past the questions in no time. You must remember to focus on your training and experience. Most of the questions in the examination will focus on real-world problems.

The Cisco Certified Network Professional and CCNA Routing and Switching is right for people who are interested in networking, they can take this examination if they have a minimum of 1 year experience in the networking business. You can work independently after CCNP and CCNA Certified examinations.

Cisco Certified Network Professional will validate that the candidate after passing this exam will be confident in planning, verifying and troubleshoot wide network areas. The candidate can also collaborate with specialist in the industry who are advanced in video, voice and wireless solutions. Achieving this certificate indicates mastery over skills that are required in enterprising roles such as network technician, support engineer, network engineer and support engineer.

The knowledge and skills on routing and switching protocol that you will gain while pursuing the Cisco Certification are an everlasting foundation for someone who has just started their career in this field or someone with years of experience. They play an important role for the network functions for the future as well as the present network.

The skills required for the role of a network engineer evolve significantly as an enterprise network gets increased amounts of demands. The field is competitive and requires IT professionals to be skilled and up-to-date with networking skills and technological advancement.

The Cisco Networking Fundamentals

The CCNA Routing and Switching Certifications will teach you about the different fundamentals of Cisco networking if you are looking to work in that field. This certification focuses on foundational IP networking skills. It also teaches individuals how to troubleshoot any issues. A CCNA certification will help you learn more about designing and configuring LAN switches, identify basic threats, configure IP routers, install and verify the basic IPv4 and IPv6 network, understand topologies, configure EIGRP, connect to a WAN, configure OSPF in IPv4 and IPv6, understand network issues and wide area of the technologies, understand device management and Cisco licensing. You will learn more about the course and some skills that will help you in your job. Your career will also improve once you obtain CCNA certification since this examination will ensure that you develop the necessary skills to perform effectively in your company. This certificate is accepted by numerous organizations since it will help you learn more about networking.

Exam Objectives

This section covers the objectives of the CCNA Routing and Switching examination.

Network fundamentals

This is the first module that is covered in the syllabus, and it includes fundamental topics like TCP/IP protocols, firewalls, etc. and others related to networks. Ipv4, Ipv6 address details are also included.

LAN Switching Technologies

In this module, different switching concepts of a network like configuring, STP protocols, inter-switch connectivity, etc. are included.

Routing Technologies

This module covers the basics of routing technology and also includes concepts about routing and the routing table. This module provides information on the types of routing like static and dynamic, routing protocols both interior and exterior, and some others like OSPFv2 for Ipv4.

WAN Technologies

This module includes a detailed study of the PPP and MLPPP configuration and verification on WAN interfaces. It also talks about the PPPoE client side interfaces that use local authentication. Options for WAN connectivity and basic QoS concepts are also included.

Infrastructure Services

Topics in this module include DNS loop operation, client connectivity issue troubleshooting, DHCP configuration and verification on routers, HSRP basics, etc.

Infrastructure Security

The topics that are covered in this module include port security, mitigation techniques for common access layer threats, traffic filtering, etc. This module also covers some information on the configuration, verification and the troubleshooting of issues that may arise during device hardening.

Infrastructure Management

This module covers the management of devices that are present in the network system. The module also covers the configuration and verification of the device monitoring protocols. It also provides information on how one can maintain the performance of the device.

Network Fundamentals

- Compare and contrast OSI and TCP/IP models

- Compare and contrast TCP and UDP protocols

- Describe the impact of infrastructure components in an enterprise network

    - Firewalls

    - Access points

    - Wireless controllers

- Describe the effects of cloud resources on enterprise network architecture

    - Traffic path to internal and external cloud services

    - Virtual services

    - Basic virtual network infrastructure

- Traffic path to internal and external cloud services

- Virtual services

- Compare and contrast collapsed core and three tier architectures

- Configure and verify IPv6 address types

- Selection of the appropriate cabling type based on implementation requirements

- Compare and contrast Ipv4 address types

    - Unicast

    - Broadcast

    - Multicast

- Comparison and contrast of network topologies

    - Star

    - Mesh

    - Hybrid

- Configuration verification and troubleshooting Ipv6 addressing

- Compare and contrast of Ipv6 address types

    - Global unicast

    - Unique local

    - Link local

    - Multicast

    - Modified EUI 64

    - Auto configuration

    - Any cast

Operation of IP Data Networks

- (SDN) Awareness of programmable network architectures.

- Recognize the purpose and function of various network devices such as Router, Switches Bridges and Hubs.

- Expanded VPN topics, DMVPN, site-to-site VPN, client VPN technologies.

- Increased focus on IPv6 routing protocols, configuration and knowledge

- Knowledge of QoS concepts.

- Select the component required to meet a given network specification.

- Understanding of cloud resources deployed in enterprise network architecture.

- Describe the purpose of the networks

- Identify common applications and their impact on the network.

- Predict data flow between two hosts across a network

- Identify appropriate media, ports, cables and connection to connect Cisco network device to other network device and host in a LAN

LAN Switching Technologies

- Configure and verify initial switch configuration including remote access management

- Determine the technology and media access control method for Ethernet networks

- Verify network status and switch operation using basic utilities such as PING, TELNET and SSH

- Identify the basic switching concepts and operation of Cisco switches

- Identify enhanced switching technologies

- Configure and verify VLANs

- Configure and verify trunking on Cisco switches

- Configure and verify PVSTP operation

- Describe how VLANs create logically separate networks and the need for routing between them

- Troubleshoot interface and cable issues (collisions, errors, duplex, speed)

- Describe and verify switching concepts

- Configure and verify troubleshoot VLANs (normal/extended range) spanning multiple switches

- Describe the benefits of switch stacking and chassis aggregation

IP Addressing – Ipv4 and IPv6

- Identify the appropriate IPv6 addressing scheme to satisfy addressing requirements in a LAN/ WAN environment

- Identify the appropriate IPv4 addressing scheme using VLSM and summarization to satisfy addressing requirements in a LAN/WAN environment

- Describe the operation and necessity of using private and public IP addresses for IPv4 addressing

- Describe the technological requirements for running IPv6 in conjunction with IPv4 such as dual stack

- Describe IPv6 addresses

IP Routing Technologies

- Describe the basic routing concepts

- Describe the boot process of Cisco IOS routers

- Differentiate methods of routing and routing protocols

- Configure and verify operation status of a device interface, both serial and Ethernet

- Configure and verify utilizing the CLI to set basic router configuration

- Configure and verify routing configuration for a static or default route given specific routing requirements

- Configure and verify OSPF (single area)

- Configure and verify EIGRP (single AS)

- Configure and verify interVLAN routing (Router on a stick)

- Configure SVI interfaces

- Manage Cisco IOS FILES

- Verify router configuration and network connectivity

- Interpret the components of a routing table

- Troubleshoot basic layer3 end to end connectivity issues

IP Services

- Configure and verify DHCP (IOS ROUTER)

- Configure and verify ACLs in a network environment

- Configure and verify NAT for given network requirements

- Configure and verify NTP as a client

- Configure and Verify Syslog

- Describe the types, features and applications of ACLs

- Describe SNMP v2 and v3

- Identify the basic operation of NAT

- Recognize high availability (FHRP)

Network Devices Security

- Configure and verify network device security feature

- Configure and verify ACLs to limit telnet and SSH access to the router

- Configure and verify Switch Port Security features

- Configure and verify ACLs to filter network traffic

WAN Technologies

- Identify different WAN technologies

- Configuration and verification of PPP and MLPPP using local authentication on WAN interfaces

- ·Describe WAN connectivity options

  - MPLS

  - Metro Ethernet

  - Broadband PPPoE

  - Internet VPN

- Configure and verify a basic WAN serial connection

- Implement and troubleshoot PPPoE

- Configure and verify frame relay on Cisco routers

- Configure and Verify PPP connection between Cisco routers

- Describe WAN topology options

- Describe the basic QoS concepts

  - Marking

  - Device trust

  - Prioritization

  - Shaping

  - Policing

  - Congestion Management

Infrastructure Services

- Description of DNS lookup operation

- Troubleshooting client connectivity issues involving DNS

- Configuration and verification of DHCP on router

    - Server

    - Relay

    - Client

    - TFTP, DNS, Gateway options

- Troubleshooting client and router based DHCP connection issues

- Configuration verification and troubleshooting basic HSRP

    - Priority

    - Preemption

    - Version

- Configuration verification and troubleshooting inside source NAT

    - Static

    - Pool

    - PAT

- Configuration and verification of NTP operating in client or server mode

Infrastructure Security

- Configuration, verification and troubleshooting port security

  - Static

  - Dynamic

  - Sticky

  - Max MAC addresses

  - Violation actions

  - Err-disable recovery

- Description of common access layer threat mitigation techniques

  - 802.1x

  - DHCP snooping

  - Non Default native VLAN

- Configuration, verification and troubleshooting of Ipv4 and Ipv6 access list for filtering traffic

  - Standard

  - Extended

  - Named

- Verification of ACLS using APIC-EM Path Trace Analysis Tool

- Configuration, verification and troubleshooting of basic device hardening

- Local authentication
- Secure password
- Access to device
    - Source address
    - Telnet/SSH
- Login banner
- Description of device security using AAA with TACAS+ and RADIUS

Infrastructure Management

- ·Configuration and verification of device monitoring protocols
    - SNMPv2
    - SNMPv3
    - Syslog
- Troubleshooting network connectivity issues using ICMP echo-based IP SLA
- Configuration and verification of initial device configuration
- Performing device maintenance
    - Cisco IOS upgrades and recovery (SCP, FTP, TFTP and MD5 verify)
    - Password recovery and configuration register
    - File system management

- · Using Cisco tools for troubleshooting and resolving problems

  – Ping and traceroute with extended option
  – Terminal monitor
  – Log events
  – Local SPAN

- Describing network programmability in enterprise network architecture

  – Function of a controller
  – Separation of control plane and data plane
  – Northbound and southbound APIs

Chapter 9

Required Learning Material
for Your CCNA Routing and Switching

❧━━━━━━━━━━━━━━━━━━━━━━━━❧

B efore you appear for an exam, it is essential to choose the right learning material. It should ideally include information about the exam, the essential questions related to the course, the exam course structure in details and the examination content. This helps the candidate to prepare well and appear for the examination. For your CCNA Routing and Switching Examination, the following are the important factors to have in mind before picking the right material.

Look Out for Free Material

While you prepare for your examination, you might have the notion that you will need the best resources to study, and may rely on expensive books and course material to learn. But many websites are currently offering study materials for this examination free of cost. Before rushing into any purchasing, conduct thorough research either online or in your organization to get the right material without having to pay any money upfront.

Your Peers are Your Greatest Resource

Nothing will compare to the knowledge a certified CCNA Network Associate can provide you. Arrange for a one-on-one session with your chosen mentor to get the right direction, and if possible, borrow their notes and books. This can be very helpful for you during the preparation. Simply address your questions to someone who has already written the examination and look ask for guidance from them.

Mix It Up

The best way to learn something is by engaging all your senses. Choose different mediums of learning, which allow you to be on your toes wanting for more, thus making your learning experience much better. Choose a mix of audios, video, text, graphics and real-time data, which will build a holistic approach of learning from personalized study material during the exam. These mix of resources will make sure you are engaged in the subject.

Keep Yourself Updated

It is always good to be updated with the current technological advancements during the exam. Make sure to keep yourself updated with the happening in the technology and network world. The study materials can only teach you so much; adding relevant information that is current along with theoretical knowledge can go a long way.

Get Practical

It is good to have part of your learning material as a practical subject. If you are already an employee of the Cisco organization, it will serve you as grounds to try and test everything that you see in order to register yourself for the practical information.

The following resources can help you gain access to the required information you need on all topics for your CCNA Routing and Switching Examination.

The Cisco Official Study Material

In the Master Exam List, under the Routing and Switching section, you will find the links towards the material and the syllabus for all the exams. Under the Routing and Switching tab, you have the ICND1 and ICND2 examination and the CCNA Composite Examination kit with all the topics that can help you prepare for the examination. Each of these exams has a percentage contribution of each topic towards the subject that cater to difficult versus easier topics. You can find the link to the master exam here.

As organizations are migrating towards a control-based framework, the role, as well as the skills necessary for a core network engineer, are rapidly evolving. This need for skills and knowledge has become more evident than ever. The CCNA Routing and Switching Certification will provide you the knowledge about the fundamental technologies and ensure that your skill sets stay relevant as this network transition takes place.

In this section, you will learn more about the study materials and the training program that you can use to complete your CCNA Certification.

Self-Study Materials

Interconnecting Cisco Networking Devices- Part 1

Interconnecting Cisco Networking Devices, Part 1 (ICND1) is an e-learning portal that's designed to assist you in preparing for the CCNA Routing and Switching Certification Exam for all the topics that are covered within the 100-105 ICND1 exam.

This course is structured such that it will provide you with a basic understanding of the network Layers 1 through 3 that are necessary for core routing and switching along with several other progressive technologies. Various topics have been included in the latest version like the information about understanding the interactions that take place and the network functioning of firewalls, wireless controllers and access points. Apart from this, you will also learn about IPv6 and the fundamentals of network security. You will be introduced to different configuration commands and to make things simpler, you will be provided different examples and related lab exercises.

This course is designed so that the training that you attain will be as effective as classroom learning. The contents of the course are available in the forms of Instructor Videos as well as text that are presented in an easy-to-understand format. Even though this is a self-paced course, it ensures interactivity via questions based on the content review, Challenge Labs with tests that are graded, and

Discovery Labs. These different aspects ensure a hands-on learning experience while simultaneously increasing the efficiency and effectiveness of the course. Apart from this, it gives the students a chance to obtain direct feedback about their understanding of the course content. To motivate the students to do better, this module provides inbuilt leaderboard and merit badges.

Upon the successful completion of this course, you will be able to:

- Define the fundamentals of networks and build basic LANs

- Secure as well as manage network devices

- Work on expanding networks that are small to medium-sized

- Be able to describe the fundamentals of IPv6

This course is specially designed for network administrators, network specialists, network support engineers and Cisco channel partners. There are no prerequisites of this course per se but having the skills and knowledge about the following topics will undoubtedly come in handy. The topics are fundamental computer literacy, essentials of PC operating system and navigation skills, primary Internet usage skills and the basics of IP addressing systems. The associated certification of this course is CCNA Routing and Switching and the associated exam is 100-1051 ICND1. English, Japanese, Chinese and Spanish are the languages supported by this module. At present, the instructional videos are available in English and Spanish.

Cisco Learning Labs for ICND1

This entire set of Cisco IOS Software labs were created to help students to prepare for their ICND1 (100-105) examination. These labs are powered by the Cisco IOS Software equipped with Layer 2 and Layer 3 features, are supported by CLI and are accessible 24/7, so, you can study and learn at your convenience. The set of labs available in this section will help you gain proficiency in configuration, management and the troubleshooting of Cisco switches and routers. This training product comes with Discovery Labs and Challenge Labs. The Discovery Labs provide guided learning so that you can learn about different concepts and the Challenge Labs will help test your understanding of all that you learn- theoretical knowledge as well as practical application of skills to further your understanding of all topics related to the CCNA Routing and Switching Certification.

This lab curriculum consists of 45 different pieces for you to go through and is in line with the learning objectives required for the 100-105 ICND1 examination. Once you clear this exam, you will be eligible for a CCENT certification.

Interconnecting Cisco Networking Devices- Part 2

Interconnecting Cisco Networking Devices, part 2 (ICND2) is an e-learning portal that is designed to assist you to prepare for the CCNA Routing and Switching Certification Exam for all the topics that are covered within the 200-105 ICND2 exam.

This is an associate-level self-paced technical course and is part of the course curriculum of the CCNA Routing and Switching Certification. It gives network administrators the necessary skills and information required for installing, configuring, operating and troubleshooting the network of a small enterprise. A couple of significant additions have been made to the existing course curriculum. These are information about Quality of Service (QoS) elements and their application, the interaction and impact of virtual and cloud services on the enterprise's network and the overview of programmability of network and associated controller types and tools available to support any network architectures that are defined by the software.

The course is structured similarly to ICND1 and upon the successful completion of this course, you will be able to:

- Work with medium-sized LANs with various switches supporting VLANs, trunking and spanning tree

- Solve problems related to IP connectivity

- Understand the configuration and troubleshooting of EIGRP in an IPv4 system and the configuration of EIGRP for IPv6

- Successfully understand the traits, functions and different aspects of WAN

- Understand the ways in which device management can be executed by utilizing conventional and smart technology

There are no prerequisites of this course per se but having the knowledge and skills about the following topics will undoubtedly come in handy. The topics are fundamental of networks, implementation of local area networks, implementation of Internet connectivity, management of devices, knowledge about securing network devices and the implementation of IPv6 connectivity. The associated certification of this course is CCNA Routing and Switching and the associated exam is 200-1051 ICND2.

English, Japanese, Chinese and Spanish are the languages supported by this module. At present, the instructional videos are available in English and Spanish.

Cisco Learning Labs for ICND2

This entire set of Cisco IOS Software labs were created to help students to prepare for their ICND2 (200-105) examination. These labs are powered by the Cisco IOS Software equipped with Layer 2 and Layer 3 features, are supported by CLI and are accessible 24/7. Again, when it comes to self-study, the module structure cannot possibly be more convenient than this. This is the second part of the ICND labs and will help you get better acquainted with configuration, management and the troubleshooting of Cisco routers and switches. Like the previous training product, this one is a combination of Discovery Labs and Challenge Labs. These two things will help you learn and then enable you to test yourself on the topics learned. This lab curriculum consists of 44 different pieces for you to go through and is perfectly aligned with the learning objectives required for the 200-105 ICND2 examination. Once you clear this exam, you will be certified for the CCNA Routing and Switching Certification.

Certification Practice Exams

MeasureUp provides Cisco Certification Practice Exams to help test your level of understanding and skills by providing you Cisco technology topics (these aren't the questions that might come in the final exam) that are related to various certification exams offered such as Cisco CCENT, Cisco CCNA Routing and Switching, Cisco CCNP ROUTE, Cisco CCNP SWITCH and Cisco CCNA Security.

Apart from this, Cisco also offers an extensive network of learning resources that include CCNA study material, CCNA Routing and Switching study sessions and access to all the latest blogs about CCNA Routing and Switching.

Training

One of the best ways to prepare for the CCNA routing and switching certification is to enroll for the different training programs that are approved by Cisco. You can enroll for either the CCNAX course or enroll for the independent courses ICND1 and ICND2.

Interconnecting Cisco Networking Devices Part 1 (ICND1)

The ICND1 course will help you learn the basics of network layers, which are important for routing and switching. You will also learn more about the basics of routing and switching which will create a base for some advanced technologies. The syllabus covered in this training module is the same as the syllabus that is covered in the

ICND1 course. Please refer to the previous section for more information about the ICND1 examination.

Interconnecting Cisco Networking Devices Part 2 (ICND2)

The syllabus or the content covered in this training module is the same as the course material you will need to prepare if you are writing the ICND2 examination. Please refer to the previous section for more information about the ICND2 examination. The difference between this training program and the self-paced learning is that the former has numerous lab exercises that you can work on to master the different training modules.

Enrollment

You can enroll for either the composite examination or the ICND1 and ICND2 examinations depending on which you choose to appear for in the following ways:

1. Choose an instructor-led training session, and enroll yourself into that session on the Cisco Learning Locator page.

2. Enroll for a private group training session on the Cisco Private Group Training.

3. Visit the Cisco Learning Network Store if you want to choose a self-paced e-learning program.

4. You should visit the Cisco Platinum Learning Library if you only want to access the digital library.

Interconnecting Cisco Networking Devices: Accelerated (CCNAX)

This course is the perfect amalgamation of the two training courses- ICND1 and ICND2. This is a 5-day training course. In this course, you will learn about the installation, management, operation, configuration and the fundamentals of the Internet Protocol version 4 or IPv4 along with the Internet Protocol version 6 or IPv6 network. Apart from all these topics, this 5-day training course will provide you information about the configuration of a LAN switch, an IP router, the ways to connect to a WAN network and the skills necessary to identify potential security breaches. This combined course will teach you about the basic troubleshooting tips and steps that are used in networks of an enterprise while preparing you for the CCNA Certification.

The different elements included in this training program are Quality of Service (QoS) as well as their applications, the effect of virtual and cloud services on enterprise networks and their interaction and a detailed overview of the network programmability along with the corresponding tools and controller varieties that are available for supporting a Software Defined Networking (SDN) architecture. The list of things you will learn from this course doesn't end. You will learn about the interactions and functions of the firewalls, wireless controller and their access point and the basics of network security and IPv6. As mentioned, this is the combination of the two courses- ICND1 and ICND2.

This course consists of instructor-led training that's spread over five days and includes lab practice too. By the end of this course, you will be able to perform all the objectives proclaimed by this course. It is appropriate for network administrators, support engineers, associate network engineers and network specialists as well as analysts. You can either enroll for an instructor-led training course or a private group training course by visiting the pages available on Cisco's official website- "Cisco Learning Locator" and "Cisco Private Group Training" respectively.

Cisco Official Course Material for Purchase

You can access all the material required to prepare for the certification examination by just paying $750. There are some topics that can be downloaded for free, while there are others that are sold at a lower price. You must ensure that you check the content and verify that the material is not repetitive.

Chapter 10

Exam Tips

You must now be aware of the different concepts and information that is covered in the CCNA Routing and Switching examination. Let us now look at some tips that will help you memorize as much as you can, and also help you perform better in your examination. You can ace the test if you create a study plan and stick to that plan. The tips in this chapter have helped many students perform well in their examinations, and I am sure they will help you perform well too.

Organize a Study Space

Create a space in your house where you will only study. If you want to ensure that you learn when you are studying, you must steer clear of any distractions. Never lie down on the sofa or bed when you are reading. You will only feel lethargic and very sleepy. You should find a table and give yourself some space to keep your books and notes. Find a comfortable chair that will prevent any backaches. You should also make sure that your phone is away from you. Do not keep your laptop close to you unless you are attending a training.

Getting rid of distractions will help you concentrate and learn better. The way people study differs sometimes. If you are someone who can focus when there is complete silence, you should study in a closed room so nobody can distract you. You might also be able to study better with some low instrumental music playing.

Get Involved in an Exam Prep Course

It is true that self-study is a bold decision to make, but it is not always the best way to study for an exam. You must understand that you need to have in-depth knowledge of the subject that you are studying if you wish to clear the exam. This is the case for entry-level certifications as well. It is important to remember that the definitions you learn for one certification may be different for another certification. Different bodies developed the study material for the exam. This means that even if you do have firsthand knowledge about the subject, some parts of the subject and sometimes the entire subject, will not necessarily be applied in the field. A task professional will use other concepts to complete the work. When you are preparing for a certification, you can spend time with an experienced professional who knows how you can beat the exam. It is always a good idea to sit with the professional and ask him or her any questions that you may have. You can also share strategies and experiences. This will improve your chances of clearing the exam.

Create Your Own Custom Study Plan

If you do not plan for your exam well, your chance of clearing the exam will drop. It is important to develop a study plan that will fit your schedule. You do not have to write an elaborate plan since a simple to-do list will also work. When you are developing your study plan, you should consider the following:

- When do you want to take the exam? You should first create your profile on the exam page, and see what location and time suits you best.

- How much time can you devote to preparing for the exam on a regular day? If you have other commitments or are working, you should ensure that you have sufficient time to cover all the topics. You should also give yourself enough time to write practice exams under exam conditions.

- Can you afford the training courses and the preparation material? You should always look for certified training and study material. This will help you develop a clear understanding of every topic that is covered in the certification. One of the best ways to ensure that you pass the exam is to purchase the pre-study material and begin reading it. This will help you create a solid foundation and also help you develop the necessary skills based on the course you have chosen.

- What training method helps you learn best? Some people love classroom sessions while there are others who prefer self-learning. Some candidates prefer online training material since they can study at any time. You should always use your experiences to help you identify the method best suited for you.

- Do you know the subject you have chosen well? It is difficult for experienced professionals who have good knowledge of the subject to clear the examination. You can use your experiences to help you understand how to tackle the examination. That being said, you should also take the questions, logic, and the length of the exam into account. When you rely only on your experiences, it can lead to bad results.

Take Practice Exams

A very effective way to prepare is taking practice exams. If there are practice exams available, you should take them and test yourself. This will not only help you assess your knowledge of the subject but will also make you familiar with how the questions are structured. It will help you in getting familiar with the format of how the questions are given. It is also recommended to time yourself while practicing so that you know how much time you take while solving each section of the paper. You will get a good idea of where you need to practice more and what requires more time. This way you can choose to deal with each section of the paper during the main exam accordingly. It is always a good idea to use official question databases and training material since that will help you emulate the real test. You should remember that you do not need to memorize every question. It may be easy to do this since there is an official question bank that is available for each certification. However, you should aim to use the practice tests as a way to identify your strengths and weaknesses.

If you notice that you do well in one area, but poorly in another area in consecutive tests, you should focus on the latter area. It is always good to use an official question database since it will not only tell you what the correct response is, but will also tell you why the other options are incorrect. This is a good way to deepen your understanding of the subject. You can also use practice exams to help you emulate the real exam. You can choose to take a set of questions when you have the time, but that does not necessarily help you since you do not solve those questions under exam conditions.

When you complete a full practice exam, you can test your attention levels, concentration, skills and resilience. That being said, you should never be discouraged when you view your practice exam results. Things will certainly go downhill when you take a practice test for the first time. This is especially true if you have not finished the course. You should take some time to study the material and ensure that you use all the available resources to improve your understanding. When you do this, you will see consistent results in your practice tests. Make sure you schedule all your practice tests long before the day you have to take the exam. You need to set the deadlines for yourself. Keep checking and track what you have learned in that period. It will allow you to take notice of any area that requires improvement.

When you take the CCNA Certification Examination, you should look at both the theoretical and practical knowledge. When you prepare for the examination, you should try your best to use all the theoretical knowledge in troubleshooting and networking issues. For example, you must know that most IP addresses are insecure. This means that you will need to identify another way to troubleshoot that vulnerability to ensure that the information passes through every node in the network. You should keep this aspect in mind when you prepare for the exam.

It is important that you understand that any CCNA Certification requires that you have some practical experience. You cannot expect to pass the exam if anyone could just grab a book and read every word that is in that book to pass. This exam is not easy, but you can improve your chances of clearing the examination if you practice some networking fundamentals. The exam does cover a lot of technology including ISP, router/switch, PC, hub and RJ-45 cords. You should start by gaining experience first in these areas before you move onto DNS, WPS and WAN. Once you understand these concepts well and know how to work with them, you can begin to build a network configuration. Once you build that network, you can see how you can troubleshoot any issues that crop up.

Another exercise that you can perform is to build network topography. All you need to do is set up a network, tear it down and build it again. Once you do this a few times, your knowledge of the foundations of networking will improve. It is important to build a lab if you want to clear the CCNA examination, and we will cover this in the next points.

Transport Layer

You should learn some common port numbers for services like Http (8), Telnet (23), Https (443) and others.

Link Layer

The data access layer focuses on Ethernet addressing. Therefore, you will need to understand the following about MAC or Media Access Control Addresses:

- A MAC address has 12 hexadecimal digits. It is a 48-bit address.

- You should also understand the MAC address table and the CAM or Computer Addressable Memory table. You should also understand how the switch uses these tables to filter or forward traffic.

- If there are two nodes or hosts on a network, they can communicate with each other using a MAC address. You should understand how the addressing works, and also understand how the host system maintains the ARP table or cache.

Study Until it Feels Like Second Nature

If you find it difficult to repeat different networking terms with accuracy, the chances of you passing your exam will decrease. The prospects will decrease further if you want to take the accelerated examination. You must remember that a CCNA examination is comprehensive, and there are some tidbits that people often overlook when studying for the exam. It is important that you learn every term that is covered in the book, and it is a lot of work to do that. You should memorize Internet speed designations, port numbers, and understand different networking tools and more. You must study every day and ensure that you commit every term that you come across to memory. Ensure that you remember the name of every item that you cover in the syllabus. You may be wondering why you need to commit everything to memory when not everything is asked in the examination. It is true that you will not be asked about every minute piece of information in the examination. That being said, you must remember that you will encounter something at work someday. A CCNA Certification is valuable since it will say a lot about your quality. You will also learn to stop mixing words and calling a router a switch.

Give Yourself a Breather

You are allowed to kick back and relax a few days before the exam, and it is what the doctor recommends. You should revise your concepts, but should not stress about it. You must ensure that you remain calm and are composed. Most students are nervous and try to cram as much information as they can during the last few days, and this is a bad idea. You should make sure that you get sufficient sleep, do not skip meals and study only when required. The last minute studying will not help you at all, and it will have a negative impact on your ability to perform well on the scheduled exam date. Give yourself a breather for a few days and rest well before the exam.

Internet Layer

Every certification exam will have a few questions about how the Internet Protocol or IP addressing works. These questions may include the following:

- It is important to know and understand the different address types in IPv6 addressing like unique local, link local and global.

- It is always a good idea to learn more about subnetting.

- It is important to understand what the subnet mask in IPv4 addressing does, and also know what the reserved address is.

Join the Online Community

When it comes to any IT certification examination, there is a lot of material that you can source from the Internet. There are numerous communities that allow you to share your experiences with the world. There are some people who want to share some examination strategies on these communities. These forums will also help you learn more about people's successes and failures. Aside from the Cisco Learning Network, you can search Google for a forum for that specific certification. You can also view the CCNA page on Reddit since there are people from across the globe that share their experiences. You must ensure that you always stay away from some toxic people and posts. There are numerous users who only use these forums to vent their frustration, and this will discourage you.

Revise

Before your scheduled exam, take time to read through the Cisco Press books and the information in this book. It will help in refreshing your memory. You will also be able to identify any portion that you may have accidentally skipped over when you first read it. This last period before taking the exam should be devoted to revising and solving more questions. You can use the various Internet forums to find any new questions that might come up on the exam. At this point, you should have ample grasp over networking concepts that are required for the CCNA certification.

Experts suggest that you should read the Cisco Press Books over and over again. This will help you ensure that everything that you have studied is fresh in your memory. You should do this before you give the actual examination. You should also identify the different concepts that are covered in the material and see if there is anything that you have missed out on. You should always dedicate the last few weeks before the exam to solving different questions and identify new questions via the mock examinations or Internet forums. It is essential to revise since you will re-learn the essential concepts that will create the foundation for the CCNA examination.

Understand TCP/IP Stack Addressing & Data Flow

When it comes to clearing the CCNA Certification, you will need to understand how the TCP/IP modern protocol stack works. You should understand how this stack is used to address different networks.

Have a Basic Understanding of the Cisco Command Line Interface (CLI)

Every Cisco Certification exam will include some lab work, and it is important that you, as a Cisco technician, have a basic understanding of the configuration and some investigative commands. Of all the commands, it is key for you to learn the commands that help you do the following:

- Examine the settings of the interface

- Verify the configuration

- View the different address tables (specifically MAC)

- Check all the routing protocols

These topics will be covered in detail in your study material, but it is always good to have some knowledge about these concepts before you sign up for the examination.

Get to Know Your Exam

It is important to know the challenge that you will face if you want to succeed. Sitting for the exam without adequate research on it will be a disadvantage for you. There are a lot of people who have given this exam, and you can benefit from their experience too. There is tons of information about the exam available on the Cisco website, and this book provides some more information about the exam. The website and book also provide useful links that will provide information on some exam topics, practice tests, study material and online tutors. This book provides an overview of the exam, including the prerequisites and the different types of questions you will face. This book also provides detailed information about the topics that you will need to know and the percentage of questions that are dedicated to each of those topics. This will help you a lot when you want to build your study plan.

Obtain the Right Material

Once you know what topics you need to study for the exam, it is time to get the right study material. The latest editions of the book are the best materials to use to prepare for the exam. These books are CCNA Routing and Switching ICND2 and CCENT/CCNA ICND1. You should also use the series called "31 Days Before." This series is available on Cisco Press. You should try to cover all the questions in this material and ensure that you can calculate in your sleep. This knowledge will help you pass your exam. Make sure you have all your notes in order and check for any handouts that your preparation center might have given. Also, take time to read over the outline of the course or the guide. You can summarize every section you learn in your own words for future reference. Getting everything together will make it easy to find the relevant material while you are studying.

Get Practical and Theoretical Experience

If you want to pass the CCNA Examination, you must ensure that you have some practical experience. You cannot expect to pass with theoretical knowledge alone. Prepare for the exam in a way that you can use the theoretical concepts for troubleshooting or networking issues in the real world. When you are aware of the problem, you must also be able to list some alternative solutions to the problem. For instance, when IP is found to be unreliable, you have to determine some alternative troubleshooting for communication between the nodes.

Never Rush to Take the Exam

You must remember that it will take you a long time before you can fully prepare for the CCNA Routing and Switching examination. These tests will include some problems that will seem like second nature to you. That being said, if you do not know some terms in the syllabus or are overconfident, you will lose some marks in the examination. You must ensure that you spread the exams out well so you have sufficient time to study. This will give you enough time to revise some concepts and also gauge if you can clear the examination with the amount of preparation that you have. You can take a less intensive route if you want to save more money. Remember that these tests have been designed to be unanswerable and tough if you have not spent sufficient time trying to understand the concepts covered in the syllabus.

Use Practice Drills and Flashcards

You may be wondering why I am asking you to use flashcards and practice drills. There are many test takers who have stated that these methods did help them pass the examination. All you need to do is make a list of all the questions that you struggled with when you were working on a mock exam. Note these questions down on flashcards and the write the answer on the back of the flashcard.

You will notice that you have a stack of cards, which you can use for your review. You should try to review these cards at least twice a day. It may bore you, and there is a possibility that it may feel like overkill, but this habit will ensure that these answers become like second nature to you. If there are some answers where you will need to perform the process, you should take some time and practice those processes until you can complete the process with no external help. This will help to drill the concepts into your head, and will also help you remember the concepts during interviews.

Have an Exam Day Preparation Plan

The examination day has finally arrived, and you are most definitely going to be anxious like every other student who is taking this examination. That being said, you should stop worrying about how the exam is going to be, and only focus on doing your best. You should ensure that you do not exhaust yourself. This section covers some simple tips that you should keep in mind.

Is your exam kit ready?

Always look at the examination website, and make sure that you have all the items that are listed on the website. The examiners are very strict, and they will ask you to leave the room if you do not have one or more of the required items with you. You must always read the exam or candidate guide and make a list of all the items that you must carry with you. Speak to the point of contact at the examination center to learn more about what you are required for you to carry with you to the examination room.

Are you calm and well rested?

This is an extremely important thing to keep in mind. Most students fail their examination because they are either physically or mentally exhausted. Students believe that they should revise every concept they can right before the exam so they can remember it. To do this, they stay up all night or wake up early on the day of the exam. What they do not understand is that it is never a good idea to read the concepts at the very last minute since it will leave you feeling anxious. If you still want to do a final review, you should try to make a list of all the concepts that you fully understand and read them before. It is never a good idea to focus on those concepts that you do not have a clear understanding of since that will cause some anxiety and panic. Alternatively, you can create a glossary or a summary to cover all the essential and necessary information. Only focus on reading the glossary before the exam. Make sure that you eat something very light before the exam.

Did you make the necessary arrangements to be on time at the test site?

There is a strict policy when it comes to time. If you are late for the examination, you may not allowed to sit for the examination. Try to leave at least an hour before the scheduled time if you use public transportation. If you own a vehicle, make sure that you identify the shortest route, and know exactly where you need to park your vehicle at the test center.

Clear your mind

You only have a little time to complete the examination. So, relax and take a deep breath before you begin answering the questions.

Remember that you have put in the required time and effort to prepare for the examination. You will not be able to do well in the examination if you overthink or are nervous.

Be aware of time

While answering the questions, you must ensure that you focus only on the question that you are working on and ignore everything else. It is always a good thing to do this since you can focus only on answering the questions correctly. That being said, you must also keep a track of time. If you have ever written an exam under pressure, you know that the time flies very quickly. Therefore, you must ensure that you have enough time left to answer the questions accurately.

Take your time reading the questions

Regardless of how much time you have left in the examination, you must ensure that you do not rush. When you do this, you can misread the question or even miss out on a question. You should always take some time out and read every question thoroughly, and also ensure that the answers you are writing are related to those questions. You should always ensure that you understand everything that is being asked in the question. This will ensure that you answer the question correctly. If you are answering a multiple choice question, you must read every option well to ensure to ensure that you do not look at the options that were put in to distract you. You should also pay attention to terms like not, never, all, least, always and most. These words will always change the meaning of the sentences. When you see a question beginning with "Choose the best answer," ensure that you read the options carefully since more than one option can be the right answer. It is recommended that you go through the exam dump before you appear for the examination since you can learn more about the different types of questions you will come across during the examination.

Try to relax

You must always ensure that you remain calm and composed during the examination. Try stretching your muscles and take deep breaths. This will help you relax your mind. When you are calm, you can always focus better, and this will make it easier for you to answer any tough question. It is important to remember that the examination you are writing is difficult, so try to have some fun while writing the examination. Trust yourself, and know that you will do great in the exam if you have stuck to your study plan. Otherwise, you will have had enough practice for the next attempt.

Keep learning

You have given the examination, and will now need to wait for five business days to go by before you receive your Certificate of Completion via email. You must understand that it is alright if you did not clear the examination. When you do not clear the examination, you are aware of the mistakes that you may have made either when you were preparing for the examination or during the examination. This means that you know what you are not supposed to do, and will be able to perform better the next time. This is an accomplishment by itself. You must always motivate yourself to perform better, since this will help you improve your chances of success. If you want to help your peers, you can share your experiences and prevent them from making the same mistakes that you did.

Remember, the CCNA exam is comprehensive. There will be questions on many varieties of topics. These will be based on studies related to TCP/IP to very comprehensive routing protocols that span trees. It may seem hard to pass the exam when you think of how much there is to study. It is recommended that you focus on ICDN1. It is usually the base for different Cisco CCNA exams. As a candidate, you will have to go through the entire breadth and length of all the topics. The exam is also very quick. It will include about 50 to 60 questions that have to be completed within 90 minutes. This short amount of time given for writing the exam can be stressful for even the most prepared person. You will, however, be able to fare well if you remember all the training you underwent and depend on your experience. The questions will mostly deal with real-world troubleshooting.

You should continue to motivate yourself and prepare well for the examination. When you are a certified CCNA expert, you can work in different organizations and can take up different roles.

Strategic Tips

Only those individuals who show the necessary skills in designing, implementing and troubleshooting different networks that are based on the TCP/IP model are awarded the CCNA Routing and Switching Certification. You must ensure that you always test your technical skills when you are preparing for the examination. A CCNA

Certification will have a great impact on your career since you may be promoted to a senior position at the organization you are working in. Let us now look at some tips you can keep in mind, apart from the tips mentioned above, to make it easier for you to pass the exam.

1. Cisco has published a blueprint for the CCNA routing and switching examination, which can be found at the following link: https://learningcontent.cisco.com/cln_storage/text/cln/market ing/exam-topics/200-125-ccna-v3.pdf. It is recommended that you go through this blueprint before you prepare for the examination.

2. Never stick to only one source when you are preparing for the examination. You should always try a combination of online trainings, videos, labs and books. This will help you learn the different concepts better.

3. It is important to remember to be honest with yourself when you talk about your understanding of the subjects. Always ensure that you know and understand a concept fully before you begin a practical assignment.

4. If you want to master troubleshooting concepts, you must learn some commands, and try to memorize them. To make it easier, you should note these commands down on a page in your book.

5. Never stick to only one workbook. You should try to look at different scenarios. As mentioned earlier, you should focus on learning more about network topologies.

6. As mentioned earlier, it is important that you always focus on reviewing your concepts, as people only retain ten percent of the information that they read.

7. You should memorize the TCP/UDP services and port numbers. This will not only help you during the CCNA examination, but will also help you during your job.

8. You should always try to look for new questions and complex questions on the Internet. Try to look at different forums and communities to collect these questions.

9. Always try to take the two-way examination. The single 200-125 CCNA examination will cost $295 while taking the 100-105 ICND1 and 200-105 ICND2 examinations will cost an additional $5 - so the total cost will come to $300.

10. You should take at least two practice examinations under examination conditions, and you should focus on the questions that you are uncertain about.

Chapter 11

Exam Study Plan

❧——◆——◆◆◆——◆◆◆◆◆——◆◆◆——◆◆❧

It is a good thing that you have decided to take up the CCNA Routing and Switching examination, and you may have started preparing for it. This book also provides sufficient information that will help you learn more about the exam. That being said, you may not have taken the time out to understand where you currently stand. You may not have created a study plan that will help you tick off the different concepts that you will need to cover while you are studying. It is important that you work on devising a study plan that will help you measure your progress. This chapter provides a four-week study plan that you can use to complete your syllabus. You can cover the entire syllabus and save some time for revision if you stick to the plan mentioned in this chapter.

You must ensure that you set aside sufficient time every day to study. According to the plan mentioned in this chapter, you must understand and complete two sections in the syllabus every week. This means that you can spend up to three and a half days on one section and the remaining time on the other. When you do this, you can ensure that you complete your syllabus in four weeks. It is important that you identify the topics that will take you some time to cover, so you can give yourself some additional time to work on those topics. You must set some time aside for practice during the fourth week, since that will help you strengthen your understanding.

You should attend a few training sessions that are available on the Global Knowledge page on the Cisco website when you have decided to study for one paper. The instructors are excellent, and they have a good understanding of the subject. These instructors may also be taking the examination at the same time as you, and will know exactly how you can clear the examination. Remember that you should understand the concepts that you are reading fully. Do not read through the syllabus just for the sake of clearing the examination.

Week 1

Every candidate will have an issue with some topics in the syllabus, but most seem to have issues with the binary and subnetting concepts that are covered in the syllabus. When you are going through your course material, it is important that you sit for the active learning sessions. You must cover the following concepts during the first week:

- Introduction to networking and the building blocks of the same, different types of networking, OSI reference and TCP/IP model

- Cabling and various types of Ethernet technologies, Cisco Layer 3 Model and the summary of the chapter

- Subnetting along with IP addressing, classes, types and composition of the IP addressing, public and private IP addresses

- Subnetting basics and variable subnet length masks, summarization of routes and troubleshooting the IP address

You can spend enough time on these concepts when you are reading through the course material. You can spend three hours or more when you are working on the different topics you must be covering during this week. Since some of the topics listed above are very short, you can spend more time on those concepts that are bigger. If you are working on a topic that is very small, you can begin to read the next topic. Do not spend this time going through the previous chapters for now. When you have covered all the topics that have been listed above, you can spend some time and verify if you can list the capabilities of the different gadgets used in the system. You can also watch numerous videos of every topic and try to read different books, which will help you understand these concepts better. You can also practice some examination questions if you have the time.

Week 2

Before you appear for the Routing and Switching Certification examination, you must clear the 640-840 examination. There are eight sections in this examination, which are listed in the syllabus, and around 76 topics are covered in these sections. During the second week, you must cover the topics listed below:

- Introduction to switches, IOS and Cisco routers, use of CLI, i.e. command line interface, the basic configuration of switches and router

- Gather the information and verify the configuration, configure the router interfaces along with DHCP and DNS and take the CCNA Lab 1 at this point

- Restoring, backing up, erasing and saving the IOS and configuration file, use of password recovery through a Cisco router, Cisco discovery and protocol and use of Telnet via IOS

- Basics of IP routing, understanding the operations of the same, default, dynamic and static routing, routing metrics and administrative details and classifying routing protocols

- Routing loops and redistribution, default route and static lab, routing protocols of RIPv2 and RIPv1, configuring, troubleshooting and verifying the RIP

- Basics to enhanced gateway interior protocol routing and configuring the EIGRP, troubleshoot and verify the same, operations and configuration of OSPF

- Redistribution and summary routes for OSP and EIGRP. You should also take the labs for EGRP, OSP and RIP at this stage

Week 3

During the third week, you should spend sufficient time in understanding the protocols. The topics that you will need to cover during this week include the switching protocol and spanning tree, understanding the configuration and functioning for catalyst switch, STP, RSTP and Ether channels with Cisco additions, Rapid spanning and VLAN spanning, BPDU guard and filter, labs for Port and STP security, MAC addressing table, VLAN and VTP, types of VLANs and Ports, VLAN trunking and protocol, Cisco firewalls and Network security, VLAN configuration and routing, device management, secure communication and security for Layer 2.

Week 4

This is the last week in your study plan, and it is important that you push yourself to work harder so you can meet your end goal. You should, therefore, work on the different topics and also practice some examination questions. You must ensure that you pull out all stops. During the fourth week, you will need to cover topics like access list and secure communication, switch port and remote access, standard and extended access list, network translation address, dynamic and static configuration of NAT, WAN and NAT troubleshooting, VPN and frame relay, IP services and IOS Netflow, NAT and WAN troubleshooting, PPP concepts and configuration, IPv6 and encryption.

Instructors and other students recommend that you should purchase the Cisco Press books if you want to take up the examination. These books will help you revise all the concepts and deepen your understanding of the subject. Ensure that you practice some examination questions, and read different forums to look for new questions.

You are now ready to take your exam! Remember to stay calm and focus only on the questions on your screen and nothing else.

Important Concepts to Learn

It is hard to clear the CCNA examination since you must have a deep understanding of the different concepts and the fundamentals of networking. When you prepare for the CCNA examination, you will need to familiarize yourself with varying concepts of networking and numerous technologies. If you want to obtain the Routing and Switching Certification, you will need to understand the concepts that are covered in both ICND1 and ICND2. That being said, there are some concepts that you must fully understand since they are the most important, as the examination will certainly ask questions based on these concepts.

TCP/IP and OSI Model

When you prepare for the CCNA Routing and Switching Examination, you must understand this topic fully since it one of the most important topics covered in the examination. The TCP/IP or Transmission Control Protocol or Internet Protocol is used by interconnecting network devices to communicate with each other. This is one of the most important concepts to understand since it is the foundation of any networking course.

The OSI or Open Systems Interconnection model is used to define the framework of any network. You can implement the different protocols in every layer of the network. It is important for you to understand the seven layers in the network. The seven layers in the OSI model are – data link layer, physical layer, presentation layer, transport layer, network layer, session layer, and application layer.

Subnetting

As mentioned earlier, it is important to deeply understand the concept of subnetting for the examination. Subnetting will help you understand how you can create two or more networks from one large network. There are two benefits to doing this:

- You can resolve any issues within the split network without affecting the whole network.

- It becomes easier to manage the network since you will only need to take care of smaller networks.

Before you give your examination, you must ensure that you know what subnetting is and also understand how it works.

IPv6

The latest version of the Internet Protocol is the IPv6, and it is a separate topic that you will need to study to clear the examination. The IPv6 is a communication protocol that gives every computer on a network its identification and location. This identification allows network administrators to manage the traffic in a network. This protocol is slightly more complex and comprehensive when compared to the Internet Protocol.

Wireless Access

You must cover all the information there is about wireless access since this technology has gained immense importance over the past few decades. It is essential that you cover this topic for your examination. Cisco offers numerous networking requirements and wireless routers, and most companies are doing their best to switch to wireless technology. Therefore, it is essential that you understand wireless access for the examination.

Network Access Translation

Network Access Translation or NAT is used when there is any information passing via a network. It will modify the information of the IP address to match the IPv4 header when it is moving in the network. The basic NAT or one-to-one NAT, as the name suggests, is the simplest NAT when compared to all the other types. This is used to interconnect two IP networks whose addresses are incompatible. This type of NAT is used by network employees and users since it supports remote accessing.

Chapter 12

Cisco Recertification

There are numerous benefits to obtaining a Cisco certification, and I am sure you are aware of how these certifications will benefit your career. There is, however, a drawback when it comes to these certifications – there is a validity period. These certifications are very different from other certifications in the sense that they expire, as the technology being used constantly changes and evolves. You cannot believe that technology will remain constant when there are innovations happening every single day. There is always some new concept added to the syllabus every year by the Cisco team, and regardless of how painful it is, you must spend some time and update yourself with the changes that are taking place to the syllabus. If you think about this carefully, you will realize that this does make sense. Cisco constantly introduces new modules or adds information to the existing modules every year. It is for this reason that every Cisco certification expires in three years or less. To ensure that you are still certified in a specific module, it is important that you recertify yourself in those modules. Let us take a look at the validity for each examination:

- All CCIE certifications and Specialist certifications expire after two years.

- The Entry, Associate and Professional-level certifications expire in three years.

- The Cisco Certified Architect has an expiry date of 5 years from the certification.

There are some charges applied towards the recertification of a module, and you will need to bear those costs. You can also obtain the recertification using other methods, and this chapter will provide further information about the same.

Certification Policy of Cisco

It isn't that good an idea to add expired certifications to your resume, but you can certainly mention them as an achievement.

Knowledge can never expire, but it certainly needs to be updated from time to time.

Entry-level certifications

If you want to renew an entry-level certificate, you'll either need to take the same exam once more or opt for a higher-level certification. For instance, if you've got a CCNA Routing and Switching Certification whose validity period is nearing expiration, you have the option to either sit for the CCNA Security examination or any other CCNA level certification exam. In the event that you are not too keen about giving an associate-level examination, you can choose to give any other professional level examination. You can choose to clear any one of the CNNP-level exams, and a certification in any of these examinations can help you recertify your basic CCNA certifications. Alternatively, you can also choose to clear the CCIE examinations. There are no prerequisites to clearing the CCIE examinations, and it is for this reason that they are easy to do. A certification in this examination will automatically help you renew your certification.

To sum it all up, the following options are available if you want to rectify or renew your CCNA certifications:

- Clear any of the present Associate-level exams except the ICNID exam

- Clear any of the present 642-xxxx professional-level or any of the 300-xxxx professional-level exams

- Clear any one of the existing 642-xxxx Cisco Specialist exams (this doesn't include Sales Specialist or Meeting Place Specialist, Implementing Cisco Telepresence Installations, Cisco Leading Virtual Classroom Instruction exams or any of the other 650-online exams)

- Clear any of the existing CCIE written exams

- Clear any of the existing CCDE written or practical exams

- Clear the Cisco Certified Architect interview along with the Cisco Certified Architect board review for the renewal of your lower certifications

You merely have to choose one of the above-mentioned options.

Professional-level certifications

As with entry-level certifications, even for professional-level certifications you have got 2 choices - either take the same exam once more or choose a certification that is at a higher-level. In this case, if you have a CCNP Routing and Switching certification whose validity period is expiring within a year, you can appear for the certification examination again or opt for a high-level examination. You can also choose to clear any other certification examination if you wish to renew the current certification that you have.

You should pass any of these options below if you want to recertify your Professional level Cisco certifications:

- Clear any of the existing CCDE written or practical exams

- Clear any of the existing CCIE written exams

- Clear any of the existing 642-xxxx professional-level or any of the 300-xxxx professional-level exams

- Clear the Cisco Certified Architect interview along with the Cisco Certified Architect board review for the renewal of your lower certifications

Expert-level certifications

Every Cisco certification has a validity period, including the expert level certifications. As mentioned earlier in this chapter, there is a constant change in technology and since these certifications are all related to technology, they need to be updated too. You must reappear for the CCIE certification examination if you want to recertify your expert –level Cisco certifications.

To renew your expert-level certifications, you must clear any of the following exams.

- Clear any of the existing CCDE written or practical exams

- Clear any of the existing CCIE written or lab exams

- Clear the Cisco Certified Architect board review and the Cisco Certified Architect interview for the renewal of your lower certifications

This is all the information you need to learn about the recertification process that you will need to follow. It is important that you recertify all your certifications before the validity of those certifications expires. You must also ensure that the time left on a certification is not added to your certification upon clearing a higher-level exam. You can track the status of your certification on Cisco's website.

Chapter 13

Sample Interview Questions and Answers

Why is it Important to Use a Switch?

A frame is created using the bits from a signal. This is done through a switch. When you do this, the switch can access or read the address of the destination. The switch will then send the frame to the correct port. A switch never broadcasts the information that it obtains in the signal across the network, and it is for this reason that this process of data transmission is very efficient when compared to other processes.

What is Routing?

Routing is defined as the process of deducing the path through which information from the source can be sent to the destination. This process is always performed using a router, which is a network layer device.

What is the Difference between IGRP and RIP?

The IGRP tries to identify the best route using which the information can be shared between the source and destination based on bandwidth, MTU, reliability and hop count. The RIP determines the best route based on the number of hops within the network.

What is MTU?

MTU or Maximum Transmission Unit is the maximum size of the packet that can be shared in the network without there being any need to break it down further.

What Purpose Does the Data Link serve?

There are two functions that are performed by the data link layer:

1. Framing

2. Verifying that the notes are passed from the source to the correct device

What is BootP?

Some organizations use networks that have a few diskless workstations that are connected to it. The network uses the Boot Program or BootP protocol to start those workstations. These diskless workstations can also use this protocol to determine the IP address of the workstation or the server.

Is a Network Divided into Smaller Sections Using a Bridge?

A bridge cannot be used to break the network into smaller segments, but it can be used to filter a large network. It does this without shrinking the network.

In What Situation Does Network Congestion Occur?

There will be a congestion in the network if there are numerous users trying to access one bandwidth. This often happens in an unsegmented and large network.

Define the Term 'Window' in Terms of Networking.

The source and destination can only share a set of segments, called the window, on any network. Once the segments are shared between the source and the destination, a notification must be sent to the source confirming that the destination has indeed received the segments.

How Many Types of Memories are used in a Cisco Router?

Every Cisco router will use the following memories:

- The NVRAM is used to store the startup configuration file

- The DRAM stores the configuration file during the execution

- The Cisco IOS is stored in the flash memory during the execution process

How Does Cut-through LAN Switching Work?

In this type of switching, once a data frame is passed to a router, it is sent out immediately and forwarded to the next segment in the network. This is done once the destination address is read.

How can you configure a Router Remotely?

There are times when you may need to configure the router remotely. One of the easiest ways to do this is to use a Cisco

AutoInstall Procedure. The router should be connected to either the LAN or WAN through at least one interface.

What Does the Application Layer do in Networking?

The following functions are performed by the application layer:

- Supports the components that are directly associated with communication in an application

- If any applications span beyond the OSI reference model specification, the application layer is used to provide network services for those applications

- Works towards synchronizing an application on the client and server side of the network

What is the Difference between the User Mode and Privileged Mode?

The user mode is used to perform a regular task when the system uses a Cisco router. These regular tasks include connecting to remote devices, checking the status of the router and to view any system information. The privileged access mode will include more options when compared to the user mode. The privileged mode can be used for debugging, including tests and making changes to the router.

Which LAN Switching Method Does the Cisco Catalyst 5000 Use?

The Cisco Catalyst 5000 uses the store-and-forward method of switching. The data frame is only shared between the source and the destination once the switch checks the CRC and saves the frame within the buffer.

Define Latency.

There are times when there is a delay between when the data is sent from one network device to another network segment. This lapse or delay is called the latency.

Define a Frame Relay.

A frame relay is used to provide connection-oriented communication by designing, creating and maintaining a virtual circuit. It is a WAN protocol. This protocol only operates at the Physical and Data Link layers and has a high-performance rating.

What is the Purpose of the LLC Sublayer?

Most application developers use the LLC or Logical Link Control sub layer to perform the following functions:

1. Error correction

2. Manage the flow of the network layer using the start and stop codes

Define HDLC.

High-Level Data Link Control or HDLC protocol is a Cisco protocol, and this is the default encapsulation that is operated in all Cisco routers.

If you want to Route an IPX, How Do You Configure a Cisco Router?

The first thing you must do is to use the command "IPX routing" if you want to enable IPX routing. Every interface within the network will then be configured or changed with an encapsulation method and network number.

What are the Benefits of VLANs?

A VLAN will allow you to create a collision domain using groups instead of just the physical location. You can establish numerous networks via different means using the VLANs. You can use different types of hardware, functions, protocols and other means to establish the network. This is one the biggest advantages of using a VLAN when compared to the LAN. In the latter the collision domain is only connected to the physical location.

Define 100BaseFX.

100BaseFX is an Ethernet, which has a data speed of 100. The main transmission medium in this Ethernet is a fiber optic cable.

Is There a Way to Switch to Privileged Mode, and What Should You Do to Switch to the User Mode?

You can enter the command "enable" if you want to access the privileged mode. If you want to move back into the user mode, enter the command "disable" in the prompt.

What Standards Does the Presentation Layer Support?

There are many standards that are used in the presentation layer which ensure that all the data in the layer is presented correctly. These standards include TIFF, JPEG and PICT for graphics and MPEG, QuickTime and MIDI for audio or video files.

List the Different IPX Access Lists.

In networking, there are two access lists:

1. Standard
2. Extended

The former access list is only used to filter the IP address of the source or destination. The latter access list filters a network using the source and destination IP addresses, protocol, socket and port.

Why do Administrators Prefer the TCP to UDP?

When compared to TCP, UDP is unsequenced and unreliable. This network cannot establish a virtual circuit or obtain any acknowledgement.

What are the Number of Hops Used When the Network Uses RIP?

If a network receives anything more than fifteen hops, it will indicate that the network or router is unreachable or out of service. Therefore, the maximum count is fifteen hops.

Define Subnetting.

Subnetting is a process of breaking a large network down into smaller networks. Since it is a part of the large network, every subnet will need to be assigned some identifiers or parameters that will indicate the subnet number.

How Can One Identify a Valid Host in any Subnet?

One of the easiest ways to do this is to use the following equation: 256 − (subnet mask). The valid hosts are found between those subnets.

What Does the Show Protocol Display?

The show protocol displays the following:

- The configured encapsulation method for every interface
- The address that is assigned to every interface
- The protocols that are routed on the configured router

How is a Cisco Router Secured? What are the Different Passwords That Can be used?

You can use five types of passwords to protect a Cisco router. The different types are:

- Terminal
- Secret
- Console
- Auxiliary
- Virtual

What are Packets?

A packet is a result of data encapsulation. The packets are data that have been encapsulated or wrapped between the different OSI layers under different protocols. They are also called datagrams.

What Process is used to create an Internetwork?

When numerous networks are connected using multiple routers, an Internetwork is created. In this network, the network administrator should assign a logical address to each network connected to the same router.

List the Advantages of Using the Layered Model in the Networking Industry.

There are many advantages to using a layered network.

- Administrators can always troubleshoot problems or issues in the network efficiently.

- The network industry is allowed to progress faster since specialization is encouraged.

- An administrator can make changes only to one layer if necessary. He or she can also ensure that this change does not affect the other layers in the network.

How Can an IP Address be depicted?

An IP Address can be depicted in three ways:

- using Dotted-decimal (for example: 192.168.0.1)

- using Binary (for example: 10000010.00111011.01110010.01110011)

- using Hexadecimal (for example: 82 1E 10 A1)

Define DLCI.

Data Link Control Identifiers or DLCI are assigned to identify every virtual circuit, and these identifiers are assigned to these circuits using a frame relay service provider. These circuits exist on the same network.

Define Segments.

A segment is a part of a data stream that moves from the top layers in OSI to the bottom layers, and towards the network. A segment is a logic unit that is found in the transport layer.

When you Configure a Router that Utilizes Both Logical and Physical Interfaces, What are the Factors that You Need to Consider When You Determine the OSPR Router ID?

A. The highest IP address of any interface.

B. The middle IP address of any logical interface.

C. The highest IP address of any physical interface.

D. The lowest IP address of any physical interface.

E. The highest IP address of any logical interface.

F. The lowest IP address of any interface.

G. The lowest IP address of any logical interface.

Correct Answer: C. The highest IP address of any physical interface.

Why Do Most Administrators Use Segmenting When They Need to Manage a Large Network?

Network administrators often use network segmenting to improve the traffic in the network. It also ensures that every user has a high bandwidth. This ensures that the network performs better. It is important to segment the network especially if it is a growing network.

What is Bandwidth?

The transmission capacity of every medium is called the bandwidth. This is used to measure the volume that any transmission channel can handle, and it is always measured in kilobytes per section.

What is the Difference between Static and Dynamic IP Addressing?

Any network is always given a static IP address manually. The dynamic IP address is given to the network via the DHCP server.

Using a Cisco Router's Identifying Information, What Are the Things That You Can Access?

You can identify the interfaces and the hostname from the Cisco router's identifying information. The former is a fixed configuration that will refer to a router port while the latter will give you the name of the router.

How Can You Access a Router?

A router can be accessed in three ways:

- Telnet (IP)
- AUX (Telephone)
- Console (Cable)

How is the Router Hold-down Timer Reset Due to a Triggered Update?

A triggered update can reset the router's hold-down timer if the timer has expired. This happens when the router receives a processing task that was proportional to the number of links present in the Internetwork.

How Do Hold-downs Work?

A hold-down will ensure that an update message does not reinstate any downed link. It does this by removing that link from that message. A triggered update is used to reset the hold-down timer.

What Command Should be Used If You Want to Delete Any Existing Configuration in a Router and Want to Reconfigure It?

A. erase startup-config

B. erase running-config

C. delete NVRAM

D. erase NVRAM

Correct Answer: A. erase startup-config

What are the Benefits of LAN Switching?

The benefits of LAN switching are:

- It allows efficient and easy migration
- It allows media rate adaption
- It allows the transmission of data through full duplex

What is the Difference between Physical Topology and Logical Topology?

The physical topology will provide the actual layout of the medium in the network while the logical topology refers to the path that the signal takes through the physical topology.

What is DHCP?

DHCP or Dynamic Host Configuration protocol is used by a router to assign the IP address to any workstation client on the network. This protocol can also be used to create a static IP address for machines like servers, printers, scanners and routers.

When You Look at the Commands Given Below, What is the Next Command that You Need to Use to Route the Traffic that is going to the Router?

Hostname: Branch Hostname: Remote

PH# 123-6000, 123-6001 PH# 123-8000, 123-8001

SPID1: 32055512360001 SPID1: 32055512380001

SPID2: 32055512360002 SPID2: 32055512380002

ISDN switch-type basic ni

username Remote password cisco

interface bri0

IP address 10.1.1.1 255.255.255.0

encapsulation PPP

PPP authentication chap

ISDN spid1 41055512360001

ISDN spid2 41055512360002

dialer map IP 10.1.1.2 name Remote 1238001

dialer-list 1 protocol IP permit

The answer is (config-if)# dialer-group 1

What is the Difference between the Hub, Router and Switch?

Routers are used to transmit the packets of data along the different networks. A switch is a tool or device that helps to filter packets or datagrams between various LAN segments. A switch can have either a single broadcast domain or multiple collision domains. A switch is used to support packet protocols, and it works in the second and third data link layers. A hub has both a multiple collision domain and a single domain. All the information that comes from one port will be sent out to another port.

Mention the Size of the IP Address.

An IP address has a size of 32 bits for IPv4 and 128s bit for IPv6.

What Does a Data Packet or a Datagram Consist Of?

A data packet or a datagram consists of the recipient's information, the sender's information and the information that is passed through the packet. The packet also contains the numeric information that will define the packet order and number. When the data is sent through the network, the information is broken down into smaller packets of data. These data packets will carry the data and the configuration for that message.

What is the Range for a Private IPS?

Ranges for private IPS are

- Class A: 10.0.0.0 – 10.0.0.255
- Class B: 172.16.0.0 – 172.31.0.0
- Class C: 192.168.0.0 – 192.168.0.255

What is EIGRP?

The EIRGP or Enhanced Interior gateway routing protocol was designed by Cisco and is used primarily on routers. This protocol will make it easier for routers to share the same route with other routers if they are all connected to the same system. EIGRP, unlike RIP, can only send an incremental update thereby decreasing the amount of data that is transferred within the network.

What Does the EIGRP Protocol Consist Of?

EIGRP protocol consists of

- MTU or Maximum Transmission Unit
- Bandwidth
- Delay
- Load
- Reliability

What is the Function of a Clock Rate?

A clock rate is used to enable the DCE or router equipment to communicate effectively.

What Command is used to Remove or Delete any Configuration Data in NVRAM?

You can either delete the configuration data, which is stored in the NVRAM in your system, or use the command erase startup coding if you want to remove that configuration data.

State the Differences Between the UDP and TCP?

UDP and TCP are two protocols that different systems use to send files across a network.

TCP (Transmission Control Protocol)	UDP (User Datagram Protocol)
TCP, a connection oriented protocol, is used to retrieve the lost part of a file. There are times when the connection may be lost when a file is being transferred. The TCP ensures that there is no data lost when a message is being transferred.	A UDP is a connectionless protocol, and when the data is sent via the network you cannot be certain that the message will reach the destination without there being any leak in the data.
This protocol will ensure that every message will reach the destination in the order that it was sent in.	The message does not necessarily have to reach the destination in the same order, which makes it difficult to use this protocol.
The data in the TCP protocol will always be read in the form of a data stream. This means that the packets in the data are always closely connected.	The packets are always transmitted independently. This makes it extremely hard for the network to ensure that the full packet has reached the destination.
Example: World Wide Web, file transfer protocol, e-mail, etc.	Example: VOIP (Voice Over Internet Protocol), TFTP (Trivial File Transfer Protocol), etc.

What is the Difference between Full Duplex and Half Duplex?

In a full duplex transmission, the communication will occur in both the directions at any given point. The transmission in a half-duplex will only happen in one direction at any point.

What is the Process of Conversion in Data Encapsulation?

The steps in data encapsulation include:

- Layer one, two and three: These are the application, presentation and session layers respectively. It is in these layers that the alphanumeric input provided by the user is converted into Data.

- Layer Four: This is the transport layer, and it is in this layer that the data is broken down into smaller chunks or segments.

- Layer Five: This is the network layer, and it is in this layer that all the data is converted into datagrams or packets. A network header is added to the data.

- Layer Six: This is the Data Link layer where all the packets or datagrams are built into frames.

- Layer Seven: This is the Physical layer, and it is in this layer that the frames are converted to bits.

If the Router IOS is Stuck, What Command Should You Use?

If the router IOS is stuck, you will need to use the following command: Ctrl + Shift + F6 and X.

Define Route Poisoning.

A route often becomes invalid because of inactivity or some suspicious activity. Therefore, it becomes important to let other points in a network know that this route cannot be used to transfer any data. The transmission can always be prevented through route poisoning.

In the Case of RIP, What Route Entry Will an Invalid or Dead Route be assigned?

If there is an RIP table entry, the invalid or dead route is assigned sixteen hops that will ensure that this network is unreachable. When any network tries to share the data using that route, the system will automatically reroute the data so it can reach the destination.

Conclusion

The CCNA Routing and Switching certification is one of the most prestigious certifications that an individual in the IT industry can earn. This book provides information about the CCNA Routing and Switching examination and also sheds some light on the other examinations offered by CCNA. This book covers some information about the different tips that you can use to ace the exam. You must ensure that you follow every word mentioned in the book to the tee. You must set aside some time to prepare for the exam because the syllabus covered is vast. If you want to clear the examination, ensure that you prepare rigorously. Your hard work will definitely pay off. This certification will let the world know that you are a networking expert. It will also prove that you have much more knowledge and expertise than any of your peers who are non-certified.

This book was written with the objective to help you understand all the details that you will need to keep in mind to clear the CCNA Routing and Switching examination. The CCNA examinations are the most difficult examinations when compared to all the other examinations one can appear for in the IT industry. This certificate will help you validate your networking skills, and will improve your career. So, make sure that you spend the required time to prepare for the examination.

If you are an aspirant of this CCNA Certification, I'm sure that this guide will help you achieve your goals. Prepare well, and do not be disheartened if you do not clear the examination in your first attempt. Try again and ensure that you do not repeat the mistakes that you made in the past.

References:

http://blog.networkbulls.com/top-5-networking-concepts-to-prepare-for-ccna-routing-switching-examination

http://index-of.co.uk/Various/CCNA%20Routing%20and%20Switching%20Study%20Guide%20-%20Lammle,%20Todd.pdf

https://career.guru99.com/frequently-asked-ccna-interview-questions/

https://learningnetwork.cisco.com/community/certifications/ccna/ccna-exam/exam-topics

https://learningnetwork.cisco.com/community/certifications/ccna/ccna-exam/study-material

https://learningnetwork.cisco.com/community/certifications/ccna/icnd2/exam-topics

https://learningnetwork.cisco.com/community/learning_center/certification_exam_topics

https://learningnetworkstore.cisco.com/on-demand-e-learning/interconnecting-cisco-networking-devices-part-1-icnd1-v3-0-elt-icnd1-v3-0-020196

https://www.bestvalueschools.com/faq/what-is-the-cisco-ccna-certification/

https://www.braindumps.com/guide-4-weeks-study-plan-for-ccna-routing-and-switching-exam.htm

https://www.certlibrary.com/blog/tips-passing-cisco-ccna-certification-exams/

https://www.cisco.com/c/en/us/products/index.html#~products-by-technology

https://www.cisco.com/c/en/us/products/switches/virtual-networking/index.html#~tab-benefits

https://www.cisco.com/c/en/us/solutions/collaboration/index.html#~stickynav=1

https://www.cisco.com/c/en/us/training-events/training-certifications/certifications/associate/ccna-routing-switching.html#~stickynav=1

https://www.cisco.com/c/en_au/products/collaboration-endpoints/index.html#~stickynav=1

https://www.cisco.com/c/en_au/products/data-center-analytics/index.html#~stickynav=1

https://www.cisco.com/c/en_au/products/hyperconverged-infrastructure/index.html

https://www.cisco.com/c/en_au/products/switches/data-center-switches/index.html#~stickynav=3

https://www.cisco.com/en/US/services/ps2827/ps2993/services_at_a
_glance_sas_sasu.pdf

https://www.cognitel.com/blog/ccna-certification/advantages-of-
ccna-certification/

https://www.globalknowledge.com/us-en/training/certification-
prep/brands/cisco/section/routing-and-switching/ccna-
routing-and-switching/

https://www.globalknowledge.com/us-en/training/certification-
prep/brands/cisco/section/routing-and-switching/ccna-
routing-and-switching/

https://www.greycampus.com/blog/networking/10-reasons-to-get-a-
ccna-certification

https://www.greycampus.com/blog/networking/everything-you-
wanted-to-know-about-ccna

https://www.greycampus.com/blog/networking/everything-you-
wanted-to-know-about-ccna

https://www.techrrival.com/prepare-cisco-ccna-200-125-exam/

https://www.urbanpro.com/ccna-certification/top-10-tips-for-ccna-
routing-and-switching

https://www.workitdaily.com/benefits-ccna-certified

https://www.workitdaily.com/benefits-ccna-certified

www.ingramcontent.com/pod-product-compliance
Lightning Source LLC
Chambersburg PA
CBHW071200050326
40689CB00011B/2200